1.15.79

Dissertations
in
American Economic History

This is a volume in the Arno Press collection

Dissertations

in

American Economic History

Advisory Editor
Stuart Bruchey

Research Associate
Eleanor Bruchey

See last pages of this volume
for a complete list of titles.

TECHNOLOGICAL ACCELERATION
AND THE GREAT DEPRESSION

Joseph Paul Waters

ARNO PRESS

A New York Times Company

New York / 1977

Editorial Supervision: LUCILLE MAIORCA

————◦◦◦————

First publication in book form, Arno Press, 1977

Copyright © 1972 by Joseph Paul Waters

DISSERTATIONS IN AMERICAN ECONOMIC HISTORY
ISBN for complete set: 0-405-09900-2
See last pages of this volume for titles.

Manufactured in the United States of America

————◦◦◦————

Library of Congress Cataloging in Publication Data

Waters, Joseph Paul.
    Technological acceleration and the Great Depression.

    (Dissertations in American economic history)
    Originally presented as the author's thesis, Cornell,
1971.
    Bibliography: p.
    1. Technological innovations--United States--History
2. Depressions--1929--United States. I. Title.
II. Series.
HC110.T4W37 1977   338.5'4'0973   76-45122
ISBN 0-405-09933-9

TECHNOLOGICAL ACCELERATION AND THE GREAT DEPRESSION

2040303

A Thesis

Presented to the Faculty of the Graduate School

of Cornell University for the Degree of

Doctor of Philosophy

by

Joseph Paul Waters

December, 1971

VITA

The author was born in Kingston, Pennsylvania, on October 7, 1944. He attended the University of Illinois where he graduated with Honors in 1966 receiving the Bachelor of Arts degree with Distinction in Economics. He was awarded a National Defense Education Act Title IV Fellowship and enrolled as a candidate for the Doctor of Philosophy degree at Cornell University in September, 1966. He has been employed as a statistical analyst by the United States Bureau of the Budget (summer, 1967), a teaching assistant in the Department of Economics, Cornell University (1968-1969), and is currently an Instructor in the Department of Economics, Middlebury College, Middlebury, Vermont. The author has been a member of Phi Eta Sigma, Omicron Delta Epsilon, Phi Kappa Phi. He is currently a member of the Econometric Society and the American Economic Association. In June, 1968, he married Carol Joyce Himes and a daughter, Heidi Jean, was born in August, 1971.

To Joyce

ACKNOWLEDGMENT

The author would like to express his appreciation to Jaroslav Vanek who originally perceived the connection between technological acceleration and the Great Depression and who proposed the present study.

Thanks are due also to John Craven and Joan Schneider who read parts of the manuscript and offered useful suggestions and to Judy Record for a thorough job of proofreading and editing. Thanks also to Mrs. Florence Finch for invaluable assistance throughout the final stages of thesis preparation.

And finally, the author wishes to express his sincerest appreciation to his wife, Joyce, for her continual patience and understanding through a most trying time.

TABLE OF CONTENTS

LIST OF TABLES

LIST OF FIGURES

Chapter I

INTRODUCTION

Statement of the Problem

The concern in post-war years, both by the mature and the underdeveloped nations, with economic growth and development has led to an extensive search for the basic determinants of growth. Economic theory suggested that increases in factor inputs were of crucial importance to increases in aggregate output. Early studies, however, soon revealed that the major impetus to economic growth was provided not by an increase in capital per worker, but rather by technological progress. Increases in inputs accounted for only ten per cent of the increase in output in the United States, the remaining ninety per cent apparently accounted for by improvements in technology.[1] Domar[2] has preferred to term this latter influence simply "the residual" and aptly so, since at the time economists had very little understanding of either the nature of technological change, the causes of improvements in technology, or the exact economic effects produced by changes in "the state of the art."

_____

[1]See, for example, M. Abramovitz, "Resource and Output Trends in the U.S. since 1870," American Economic Review, XLVI (May, 1956); and R. Solow, "Technical Change and the Aggregate Production Function," Review of Economics and Statistics, XXXIX (August, 1957), reprinted in M.G.Mueller, ed., Readings in Macroeconomics (New York: Holt, Rinehart and Winston, Inc., 1967), pp. 323-333.

[2]E. Domar, "On the Measurement of Technological Change," Economic Journal, LXX (December, 1961)

1

With the discovery of the crucial role played by
technology, economists began devoting an increasing amount of
time and effort   to the study of technological change.[3]
Research in this field has divided itself along three major
lines: empirical estimates of the actual rates at which technology has advanced,[4] studies into the causes of technical
progress,[5] and the incorporation of technical change into
macroeconomic models of the economy.[6] The present study falls
under the third category although it is inspired by results
obtained in empirical studies of technical progress covering
the first half of the twentieth century in the United States.

Much of the work attempting to include technology
parameters in macroeconomic models has been concerned with
long-run implications. The primary reason for this development

[3]For an excellent review of the literature on technological change and an extensive bibliography see L. Lave, Technological Change: Its Conception and Measurement (Englewood
Cliffs, N.J.: Prentice-Hall, Inc., 1966).

[4]Appropriate references are cited in the next section of
the present chapter.

[5]E. Denison, The Sources of Economic Growth in the U.S.
and the Alternatives Before Us (New York: Committee for Economic
Development, 1962); C. Carter and B. Williams, Industry and
Technical Progress (London: Oxford University Press, 1957),
Investment in Innovation (London: Oxford University Press,1958),
Science in Industry (London: Oxford University Press, 1959);
R.Nelson,ed., Rate and Direction of Inventive Activity, National
Bureau of Economic Research(Princeton: Princeton University Press,
1962).

[6]For a survey of the literature on economic growth see
F. Hahn and R. Matthews, "The Theory of Economic Growth: A
Survey," Economic Journal, LXXIII (December, 1964).

is the relative difficulty of including technical change in
a short-run framework. Economic growth models, which are by
their very nature restricted to long-run analysis, have been
able to incorporate technology through such devices as the
measurement of inputs in terms of "efficiency" units or by
the embodiment of improved technology in new capital equipment.[7] Short-run models, however, have generally assumed an
invariant technological structure. Indeed, the current framework of short-run Keynesian models does not lend itself to an
inclusion of technological parameters. Improvements in technology are generally reflected in an increased capacity to
produce or in shifts of the aggregate supply curve. Current
short-run models, being basically demand-oriented, pay little
attention to movements in aggregate supply. Investment, of
course, is recognized as a critical variable, but its role in
increasing capacity is often ignored. The rationale given for
this exclusion of supply effects is that the flow of investment
in the short-run produces such a negligible effect on the
aggregate capital stock that capital, and hence capacity output,
can be regarded as constant. Unfortunately, this approach
makes all but impossible any analysis of the mutual interaction
between technology, investment, full-capacity output, and
aggregate demand.

---

[7]Lave, op. cit., provides a useful bibliography covering
the capital and growth models. p. 113.

Technology is certainly not static. Yet if it could be assumed that the rate of technical progress is relatively constant, then the above limitations of current short-run models would be of little importance. However, empirical studies attempting to measure the rate of technological progress have indicated that the growth rate of technology, although constant for certain time spans, is subject to major fluctuations. One such fluctuation in the rate of technological advance occurred sometime during the decade of the 1920's. An acceleration in the rate of technical progress resulted in a doubling of the annual rate of technical advance from 1 % per year to 2 % per year. This acceleration in the rate of technical change takes on added significance when it is recalled that after the decade of the 1920's came the decade of the 1930's and the greatest depression the country had ever experienced. The question naturally arises: What part, if any, did this acceleration of technical change play in the development of the disequilibrium in the American economy which led to the Great Depression?

If there is any connection between the acceleration in technology and the Great Depression, then it is imperative that this connection be understood. Major technological breakthroughs leading to an acceleration similar to that which occurred in the 1920's are quite likely to occur again. In fact, the current development of innovations such as the computer, nuclear power, and the beginnings of the space age

promise as yet undreamed of advances. If an acceleration in
technology produces, not only a considerable increase in output, but also a violent disequilibrium in the structure of
production, then it is obvious that even the short-run
Keynesian models should be capable of incorporating the
effects of a changing technology into their analysis. Even
if the doubling in the rate of technical progress played a
minor role in the events leading to the Great Depression,
nonetheless, the fact that the rate of progress is subject
to change indicates that a more general Keynesian framework
is required. This study is an attempt to provide such a
framework.

The Evidence of Acceleration

Since this paper will be based on the assumption that
a technological acceleration did, in fact, occur, it would be
wise at the outset to review the evidence upon which this
assumption is based. Although Robert Solow was the first to
draw attention to the evident break in the trend of technological progress,[8] Jacob Schmookler's earlier study, "The Changing Efficiency of the American Economy, 1869-1938," contains
results consistent with later research.[9] Table I repeats
Schmookler's estimates of output per unit of input for over-

---

[8]Solow, op. cit., p. 328

[9]Review of Economics and Statistics, XXXIV (August, 1952).

TABLE 1

SCHMOOKLER'S ESTIMATES OF EFFICIENCY AND CORRESPONDING

ANNUAL RATES OF CHANGE, 1894-1938.

Period	Output per unit of input[a] (1)	Average Annual Rate of Growth	
		5-yr. intervals (2)	longer (3)
1894-03	.664		
		1.20%	
1899-08	.705		
		1.22	
1904-13	.749		0.9%
		0.74	
1909-18	.777		
		0.66	
1914-23	.803		- - -
		2.60	
1919-28	.913		2.0
		1.35	
1924-33	.977		
		0.87	
1929-38	1.020		

[a]Data taken from J. Schmookler, "The Changing Efficiency of the American Economy, 1869-1938," Review of Economics and Statistics, XXXIV (August, 1952), Table 9., column (4), p. 226. The labor input for this series is measured in terms of manhours.

lapping decades from 1894 to 1938. The average annual rates
of growth implied by these estimates are given in column (2).
The most striking increases arise in the years between 1919
and 1924 when the efficiency of the American economy was
increasing at over. $2\frac{1}{2}$ % per year. The breakdown of time by
overlapping decades is to some extent arbitrary. Therefore,
to provide an estimate of the rate of technical progress
comparable with periods used in other studies, the annual
rate of improvement for the periods 1899-08 to 1914-23 and
1914-23 to 1924-33 is computed and given in column (3).
Taking these longer time spans into account transforms
Schmookler's results into a form almost identical with later
research. The rate of technical progress is approximately
1 % per year prior to 1919 and then accelerates to approximately
2 % per year in the years following 1919.

In his 1957 paper, Solow attempted to segregate variations in per capita output due to changes in the capital-
labor ratio from those due to technological change. Solow's
measure is derived on quite general assumptions.[10] Production
is assumed to be a function of capital, K, labor, L, and
technology, represented by the variable t for time. Solow

_____

[10]For a criticism of Solow's method and a correction of
an arithmetical error in the original paper see W. P. Hogan,
"Technical Progress and the Production Function," Review of
Economics and Statistics, XL (November, 1958)(followed by
Solow's reply); and H. Levine, "A Small Problem in the Analysis
of Growth," Review of Economics and Statistics, XLII (May, 1960).

assumed that technical change has been, on the whole, neutral; a change in technology tending to leave the ratio of the marginal products of both factors unaffected.[11] The production function is, therefore, represented by equation (1.1) where the multiplicative factor $A(t)$ measures the cumulative effect of shifts

$$(1.1) \qquad X = A(t)f(K,L)$$

in the production function over time. Without specifying an explicit form for the production function, if the additional assumptions of constant returns to scale in production and the equality of factor prices with marginal products are made, the $A(t)$ series can be estimated.

Differentiating equation (1.1) with respect to time and dividing by output yields an expression for the rate of growth of output, equation (1.2). In equation (1.2) the dot over a

$$(1.2) \qquad \dot{X}/X = \dot{A}/A + f_k \dot{K}/f(K,L) + f_l \dot{L}/f(K,L)$$

variable indicates the derivative with respect to time while the expressions f_k and f_l represent the partial derivatives of

---

[11] The definition of neutrality has been a subject of some controversy. See J. Hicks, The Theory of Wages, second edition (New York: St. Martin's Press, 1966); J. Robinson, "The Classification of Inventions," Review of Economic Studies, V (February, 1938); W. Salter, Productivity and Technical Change, (Cambridge: Cambridge University Press, 1960); H. Uzawa, "Neutral Inventions and the Stability of Growth Equilibrium," Review of Economic Studies, XXVIII (February, 1961); C. Kennedy, "Technical Progress and Investment," Economic Journal, LXX (June, 1961) and "The Character of Improvements and of Technical Progress," Economic Journal, LXXII (December, 1962); A. Asimakopulos, "The Definition of Neutral Inventions," Economic Journal LXXIII (December, 1963).

the production function with respect to capital and labor respectively. By multiplying and dividing the second term on the right by K and the third term by L, and recalling that marginal products are assumed equal to factor costs, equation (1.2) is transferred into equation (1.3) where W_k represents capital's share in output and W_l labor's share. Since factor

$$(1.3) \qquad \dot{X}/X = \dot{A}/A + W_k(\dot{K}/K) + W_l(\dot{L}/L)$$

shares add to unity, labor's share can be eliminated from the equation. Finally, by denoting the capital-labor ratio by k and per-capita output by x, Solow's final estimating equation is derived. All that is needed to estimate a series represent-

$$(1.4) \qquad \dot{x}/x = \dot{A}/A + W_k(\dot{k}/k)$$

ing the rate of growth of technology is data on per capita output, the capital-labor ratio, and capital's share in output. Given the series A/A, $A(t)$ can be constructed by simply assuming an initial value of unity: $A(0) = 1$.[12]

Although the data employed by Solow has been criticized, his results did provide one of the first indications of the movements of technology in the American economy.[13] They also

----

[12]Domar, op. cit., illustrates how the Solow method can be interpreted as a geometric rather than an arithmetic index of technical change.

[13]B. Massell, "Capital Formation and Technical Change in U.S. Manufacturing," Review of Economics and Statistics, XLII (May, 1960) has reestimated Solow's index using more recent data and including only the manufacturing sector. His results closely parallel those obtained by Solow.

revealed the apparent acceleration in the rate of technical
progress. Solow noted:

> There is some evidence that the average rate of
> progress in the years 1909-30 was smaller than that
> from 1930-49. The first 21 relative shifts average
> about 9/10 of one per cent per year, while the last
> 19 average $2\frac{1}{4}$ per cent per year. Even if the year
> 1929, which showed a strong downward shift, is moved
> from the first group to the second, there is still a
> contrast between an average rate of 1.2 per cent in
> the first half and 1.9 per cent in the second. Such
> post hoc splitting-up of a period is always dangerous.
> Perhaps I should leave it that there is some evidence
> that technical change (broadly interpreted) may have
> accelerated after 1929.[14]

The date separating the two periods suggested by Solow differs
by nearly ten years from that suggested by other studies. This,
perhaps, is influenced by the fact that his study begins in
1909. Other investigators fix the date for acceleration
much closer to the beginning of the decade. If the rate
of progress computed for the period 1909 to 1920-21 is compared with that for the period 1920-21 to 1939-40 using Solow's
data, the average annual rate of technical change is seen to
jump from 0.8% in the first period to 1.9% in the second.
Thus, in spite of the fact that Solow observes the break in
trend near 1929, his data is consistent with observations
placing the break much nearer to 1920. Considering the
tremendous increases in productivity which occurred during

---

[14]Solow, op. cit., p. 328.

the 1920's, it is more likely that the acceleration preceded
the improvements in per capita output.

The first major investigation to confirm the acceleration in technical change noted by Solow is found in the study
of productivity trends compiled by John Kendrick in 1961.[15]
Kendrick employs an arithmetic index in constructing his
productivity ratios. Defining productivity as "the ratio of
real product in the economy or in component industries (pre-
ferably at constant unit factor cost) to the associated real
national income deflated by factor prices,"[16] Kendrick com-
putes his productivity ratios by weighting outputs and factor
inputs in any given year (II) by the prices and factor costs
of a given base year (I). The meaning of a change in such
productivity ratios is explained by Kendrick:

> We are comparing what the outputs of II would
> have cost at the factor prices and unit factor re-
> quirements of I (real output) with what they did
> cost in constant I factor prices but at the II level
> of productive efficiency (real input). Alternatively,
> we are comparing the actual real output of II with
> what the output of the factors would have been in II
> had the productive efficiency of I (real input) pre-
> vailed.[17]

Productivity ratios computed in this manner are likely to be

---

[15]J. W. Kendrick, Productivity Trends in the United States,
(Princeton: Princeton University Press, 1961). For an earlier
report and summary of Kendrick's results see S. Fabricant, Basic
Facts on Productivity Change, National Bureau of Economic Research
(New York: Columbia University Press, 1959).

[16]Kendrick, op.cit.,p. 10.   [17]Ibid., p. 11.

sensitive to the actual degree of capacity utilization in production. To minimize this effect, Kendrick based his analysis of productivity trends on the estimates of productivity in "key years" when economic activity was at a high level. These productivity trends thus reflect the long-run effects of "innovation on the organization and technology of production, including that induced by changes in scale."[18]

Kendrick's study covered the period between 1889 and 1957. During these years total factor productivity increased at an average annual rate of approximately 1.7 per cent,[19] although the break in trend was clearly evident:

> Examination of the annual index numbers of total factor productivity reveals a distinctly higher trend since World War I than that which prevailed in the three prior decades. Rates of growth computed between the terminal years of the two periods are 1.3 per cent a year for 1889-1919 and 2.1 per cent for 1919-57. Actually, the change in trend could be interpreted as beginning in 1917, but it is more convenient for us to use the key year 1919 as the dividing point. The results are not substantially affected.[20]

The studies of Schmookler, Solow, and Kendrick all employ an index number of one form or another to measure technical progress. More recent work has attempted to measure technical progress by directly estimating an aggregate produc-

---

[18]Ibid., p. 12

[19]Compare this with the 1.5% obtained by Solow and the 1.3% implicit in Schmookler's work.

[20]Kendrick, op. cit., p. 65.

tion function. Many of the studies employing this method have
concentrated on individual sectors in the economy and have
spanned more recent periods,[21] and thus can not add to the
evidence of acceleration in the 1920's. Murray Brown, however,
provides an estimate of technological change in the United
States for the period 1890 to 1960. By employing a Cobb-
Douglas production function, Brown seeks to isolate "technological epochs," periods in which technology has remained
invariant. It is significant that the years 1920-1921 mark a
break between two separate epochs:

> Three structural breaks in the Cobb-Douglas
> production function in the private domestic non-farm
> sector are evident in the overall period 1890-1960.
> They are dated roughly between 1906 and 1907, 1920
> and 1921, and between 1939 and 1940. These breaks
> permit us to define, approximately, four technological
> epochs. They are 1890-1906, 1907-1920, 1921-39, and
> 1940-1960.[22]

Quantitatively, Brown's estimates of neutral technological change are consistent with earlier observations.
For the period 1921-1939, Brown estimates that technology
advanced at the rate of two per cent per year.[23] When com-
paring technological progress in the period 1890 to 1921 with

---

[21]Lave, op. cit., provides a bibliography of estimates
of technical change for United States manufacturing, agriculture,
and services in addition to studies of foreign countries. p. 46.

[22]M. Brown, On the Theory and Measurement of Technological
Change, (Cambridge: Cambridge University Press, 1966), p. 152.

[23]Ibid., p. 159.

1921 to 1960, Brown concluded that "the effect of total neutral technological progress rose roughly by a factor of 5 from the first comparison period to the second."[24] If the effects of non-neutral technological progress are included to determine the total impact of changing technology, a substantial rise is still evident between the two periods, the rate of progress after 1921 being $2\frac{1}{2}$ times the pre-1921 rate.[25]

Yet a fourth estimate of technological change can be obtained by combining Jaroslav Vanek's model of economic growth, which explicitly includes technological change, with the data calculated by Kendrick.[26] Consider an economy subject to a linearly homogeneous production function with Hicks' neutral technical change constant at the rate α. The variables X, K, and N represent real output, capital, and labor inputs respec-

$$(1.5) \qquad X = Ae^{\alpha t}F(K,N)$$

tively in equation (1.5). The rate of growth of the employed labor force is assumed to remain constant at $\underline{n}$. Since (1.5) is linearly homogeneous, it can be represented in per-capita terms. Using an asterisk to represent per-capita variables, equation (1.6) can now be used to derive a fundamental relation

$$(1.6) \qquad X* = Ae^{\alpha t}f(K*)$$

---

[24]Ibid., p. 161.   [25]Ibid.

[26]J. Vanek, "A Theory of Growth with Technological Change," American Economic Review, LVII (March, 1967).

between the rates of growth of per-capita income and the
capital-labor ratio. Differentiating (1.6) with respect to
time and dividing by X* yields the rate of growth of per-
capita income, x*. Defining the rate of growth of capital
by equation (1.7) and that of labor by (1.8), the rate of growth

(1.7) $\qquad k = \ddot{K}/K$

(1.8) $\qquad n = \dot{N}/N$

of per-capita income is given by equation (1.9) where k*
represents the rate of growth of the capital-labor ratio. The

(1.9) $\qquad x^* = \alpha + \phi_K k^*$

term ϕ_K ($= K^*f'/f$) represents capital's share in output.
With constant returns to scale, capital's share and labor's
share, ϕ_N, will sum to unity.

By a simple rearrangement of equation (1.9), an equation
can be derived which yields a separate estimate of the rate of
technical progress, α, provided only that data on the rate of
growth of per-capita income, the capital-labor ratio, and

(1.10) $\qquad \alpha = x^* - \phi_K k^*$

capital's share in output are available. Capital share data
as well as the data necessary to calculate the relevant rates
of growth have been provided by Kendrick's study and are
reproduced in Appendix Tables I - V.[27]

---

[27]Vanek measures technological change by using an
"equilibrium equation." Assuming a constant savings rate

and the usual equality of savings and investment, the rate of growth of capital can be defined by (i). To examine the move-

(i) $\qquad k = s_0 X^*/K^*$

ment of the rate of growth of capital over time, differentiate equation (i) with respect to time:

(ii) $\qquad \dot{k} = k(\alpha - \phi_N(k-n))$

When $\dot{k} = 0$, the rate of growth of capital will remain constant. Setting equation (ii) to zero and solving for k yields the asymptotic rate of growth of capital, $\bar{k}$:

(iii) $\qquad \bar{k} = n + \alpha/\phi_N$

If the rate of technical progress and the rate of growth of labor and labor's share in production are constant, then $\bar{k}$ will be constant. It is easy to show that any rate of growth of capital not initially equal to the asymptotic rate will gradually approach that rate. To see this, note that equation (ii) can be rewritten in the form,

(iv) $\qquad \dot{k} = k \phi_N(\bar{k} - k)$.

If the actual rate of growth of capital, k, exceeds the asymptotic rate, then the derivative of k with respect to time is negative and the rate of growth of capital must be declining toward the asymptotic rate. On the other hand, if k is initially below $\bar{k}$, the derivative will be positive and k will be increasing toward $\bar{k}$.

If the economy has reached the asymptotic rate of growth, then the rate of growth of per capita income will be constant and equal to the rate of growth of the capital-labor ratio:

(v) $\qquad \overline{x^*} = \overline{k^*} = \alpha/\phi_N$

Vanek's "equilibrium equation" then is simply:

(vi) $\qquad \alpha = x^*\phi_N$

Unfortunately, this equation holds only when the economy has attained the asymptotic rate of growth, or when x^* is equal to k^*. In the period under consideration this has generally not been the case. Nevertheless, the estimates of the rate of technical progress given by using Vanek's equilibrium equation are provided in Appendix Tables II and III. To estimate the actual difference between k and $\bar{k}$, define:

(vii) $\qquad k = \bar{k} + \gamma = n + \alpha/\phi_N + \gamma$

(viii) $\qquad \gamma = -(x^* - k^*)/\phi_N$

Equation (viii), derived from equation (vii), can be used to provide an estimate of precisely how close an economy is to its asymptotic growth rate. These estimates are available in Appendix Tables II and III.

Table II below provides estimates of α in addition to the relevant growth rates and factor shares for selected time periods. For comparison, the rate of growth of Kendrick's series on total factor productivity have been included. The calculated growth rates are remarkably close to Kendrick's factor productivity growth rates and serve to confirm the break in the trend of technological progress after 1919.

TABLE II

GROWTH RATES OF MAJOR VARIABLES, SELECTED YEARS, 1889-1957.

Time Period	Capital's Share ϕ_K	Rate of Growth			
		Per-Capita Income x*	Capital-Labor Ratio k*	Technical progress α	Factor Productivity
1889-1919	.29	1.6	1.1	1.3	1.3
1919-1953	.24	2.3	0.7	2.1	2.1
1889-1899	.30	2.0	1.6	1.5	1.6
1899-1909	.29	1.3	0.5	1.2	1.2
1909-1919	.28	1.5	1.2	1.1	1.1
1919-1929	.28	2.2	0.8	2.0	2.0
1929-1939	.24	2.1	1.1	1.9	1.9
1939-1949	.23	2.1	-0.1	2.2	2.2
1949-1957	.19	2.9	2.5	2.4	2.3

The fact that four entirely different approaches to the measurement of technical progress have all arrived at the same conclusion, that the rate of technical change increased from approximately 1% per year prior to 1920 to approximately 2% per year after 1920, lends convincing evidence to the assumption made in this paper that an acceleration in the rate of technical progress did, in fact, occur.[28] Brown

concluded that the next step in the analysis is the explanation
of this acceleration:

> The expansion of the acceleration in neutral tech-
> nological advance from the earlier to the later part
> of the period under consideration is a problem of
> first importance. For until an adequate explanation
> is forthcoming, this component of growth is not amen-
> able to control; it follows from the large influence
> neutral technological progress has on economic growth
> that the process of growth itself is not amenable to
> control until an acceptable explanation evolves.[29]

Not only is the process of growth largely uncontrollable,

a long-run concern, but efforts at economic stabilization will

be subject to error if either the causes or the effects of the

acceleration remain unexplained. Although an attempt is

made in this study to outline the probable causes of the

acceleration in technology, the principal effort is directed

toward evaluating the probable short-run consequences. To

accomplish this task a model must be constructed consistent

with observed long-run growth and irregular short-run cyclical

fluctuations. It must be capable of analyzing unemployment of

either capital or labor, the impact of changing factor prices,

the effect of autonomous shifts in aggregate functions or

---

[28]It might be added that Brown and Popkin in an earlier
study of the 1890-1958 period uncovered two structural breaks
one occurring between 1918 and 1919 and the other between 1937
and 1938. M. Brown and J. Popkin, "A Measure of Technological
Change and Returns to Scale," Review of Economics and Statistics
XLIV (November, 1962).

[29]Brown, op. cit.,pp. 162-63.

monetary variables, and, of course, the likely results of
technological changes. Needless to say, the complexity of
this problem defies any simple, or for that matter complicated,
mathematical model. The answer to the question, What is the
likely short-run effect of an acceleration in technology? is
It all depends. It all depends on how the parameters in the
system are moving. If the acceleration in technology is
accompanied by a massive contraction of the money supply, the
effect is likely to be quite different than if it is accompanied by an expansion in the money supply. The model
developed here, thus, provides only a framework in which
short-run movements of the economy can be analyzed. The
reader is, therefore, cautioned not to look for a "final
equation" specifying the time path of all the variables in
the system from now until infinity. Such an equation simply
does not exist.

Organization of the Study

The basic model is constructed in Chapters II through V,
while Chapters VI through VIII provide applications of the model.
Chapter II is concerned with the development of an aggregate
supply curve and its relationship to the production function
and other parameters of the system. The critical link between
the position of the aggregate supply curve and the existing
capital stock, a consideration largely ignored in current
derivations of the aggregate supply curve, is explained in some

detail. The concept of aggregate demand is considered in
Chapter III. The various definitions of aggregate demand
advanced in the literature are explored and the concept
most useful to short-run analysis chosen. The consumption
function is discussed and, with investment for the moment
assumed constant, the determination of the aggregate price
level and the actual rate of real output is illustrated.

The key to any short-run model is, of course, the
investment function. Based on very general assumptions of
profit maximization and perfect competition, a non-linear
aggregate investment function is derived in the fourth Chapter.
The rate of gross investment expenditures is seen to be a
function of current factor prices, the rate of technical
change, and the relationship between current output rates
and optimal output rates as determined by the parameters of
the system and the existing stock of capital. In the process
of derivation, an investment function similar to that developed
by Kaldor[30] and also by Vanek[31] is encountered. However, when
certain simplifying assumptions are relaxed, both the form and
implications of the investment function are radically altered.
Chapter V summarizes the short-run model and discusses the

---

[30]N. Kaldor, "A Model of the Trade Cycle," Economic
Journal, XLIX (March, 1940).

[31]J. Vanek, "The Labor Market, Technology, and Stability
in the Keynesian Model," Kyklos, XVI (1963).

relationship between short-run and long-run functions in the system. The effects of changes in the parameters assumed constant and the growth potentialities of the system are explored in this chapter.

The application of the model to business cycle theory is illustrated in Chapter VI. It is found that most of the current theories of the cycle can be explained within the framework developed in the earlier chapters if the appropriate parametric assumptions are made. Before the model is applied to the events of the 1920's, Chapter VII provides a discussion of the principal technological developments leading to the acceleration in the rate of technical progress. Of key importance in this regard are the development of new industries during the period and the evolution of major institutional innovations. Finally, Chapter VIII applies the model to a discussion of the events leading up to the Great Depression and attempts to illustrate the role played by technology as well as the other components of the system. It is demonstrated here that the acceleration in technical change did, indeed, play a role in causing the Great Depression. However, that role was conditioned by simultaneous movements in aggregate demand during the 1920's which allowed the economy to drift into an unprecedented position of disequilibrium and by a severe contraction in the money supply after the crash.

Chapter II

THE PRODUCTION FUNCTION AND AGGREGATE SUPPLY

The Derivation of Aggregate Supply

Textbook descriptions of the Keynesian macroeconomic
system often provide extensive analysis of the determinants
of aggregate demand while ignoring the question of aggregate
supply. In this study emphasis is placed primarily on the
effects technological change is likely to have on investment
decisions. These, in turn, are crucial to movements in the
capital stock and hence production and output. For this
reason, the analysis begins by considering first an aggregate
production function and the derived aggregate supply curve.

The development of this chapter is basically neoclassical in origin.[1] An aggregate production function is
assumed to exist[2] relating the flow of final output to the

---

[1] For a complete and detailed treatment of the modern
neo-classical theory of production see C.E.Ferguson, The
Neoclassical Theory of Production and Distribution, (Cambridge:
Cambridge University Press, 1969).

[2] There has been some controversy over whether any such
aggregate production function does, in fact, exist. The
position adopted here is that if not an explicit function, at
least a "surrogate production function" can be assumed to
exist. See J. Robinson, "The Production Function," Economic
Journal, LXV (1955); P. Samuelson, "Parable and Realism in
Capital Theory: The Surrogate Production Function," Review of
Economic Studies, XXIX (June, 1962). For a discussion of the
conditions under which an aggregate production function exists
see H. Green, Aggregation in Economic Analysis, (Princeton:
Princeton University Press, 1964). An excellent review of

stock of capital and to the flow of labor services. Labor, L,

and real output, X, are viewed as flow variables while the stock

of capital, K, represents a given quantity of physical goods.

The lead of Vernon Smith is followed here in defining the

distinguishing characteristic of the "capital good", namely:

its presence is required if output is to be produced at all.[3]

The long-run production function is thus given by equation (2.1)

where the subscript t refers to the tth time period. The

(2.1) $X_t = X_t(K_t, L_t, A_t)$

variable A represents an index of the level of technology or

state of the art. Equation (2.1) is viewed as a long-run

production function since it allows both the level of tech-

nology, A_t, and the stock of capital, K_t, to vary. In the

short-run, technology and the stock of capital are given

constants. Equation (2.2) gives the short-run production

function:

(2.2) $X_t = X_t(K_o, L_t, A_o)$

---

empirical studies of the production function is provided by
A. A. Walters, "Production and Cost Functions," Econometrica,
XXXI (January, 1963).

[3]Many writers prefer to regard the capital input as a
flow of services just as the labor input represents a flow of
services. The view adopted here derives mainly from the work
of V. Smith, "The Theory of Investment and Production," Quarterly
Journal of Economics, LXXIII (February, 1959), "Problems in
Production-Investment Planning Over Time," International Economic
Review, I (September, 1960); and Investment and Production: A
Study in the Theory of the Capital-Using Enterprise, (Cambridge:
Harvard University Press, 1960).

If a well-behaved[4] production function is assumed, equation (2.2)
can be illustrated graphically by the usual total product of
labor, and marginal product of labor curves depicted in Fig. 1.
This is the formulation most often employed in describing
either the Keynesian or the Classical systems. When the
assumptions of perfect competition, profit maximization, and
a fixed money wage rate are added, it is a simple matter to
derive an "aggregate supply curve."[5]

Firms maximize profit if production is carried to the
point where marginal revenue is just equal to the marginal
cost of production. Under perfect competition, marginal
revenue is equal to average revenue which is simply the price.
With labor the only variable input, marginal cost is equal to
the money wage rate, W, divided by the marginal physical
product of labor (MP_L). Thus, the profit maximizing condition
in the short-run can be stated as the equality of the price

---

[4]A production function is defined as "well-behaved" if
it satisfies the following conditions: (1) $X(0) = 0$,
(2) $X(\infty) = \infty$, (3) $\delta X/\delta L > 0$, and (4) $\delta^2 X/\delta L^2 < 0$.

[5]This type of "aggregate supply curve" relating prices
to output or the closely related version which relates output
and/or employment to aggregate expenditure can be found in
N. Keiser, Macroeconomics, (New York: Random House, 1971), p.303;
E. Shapiro, Macroeconomic Analysis, 2nd. ed., (New York:
Harcourt, Brace & World, Inc., 1970), p. 320; J. Lindauer,
Macroeconomics, (New York: John Wiley & Sons, Inc., 1968),
pp. 197-209; P. Davidson and E. Smolensky, Aggregate Supply
and Demand Analysis, (New York: Harper & Row, 1964), Chap. 9,
pp. 117-35; and J. McKenna, Aggregate Economic Analysis, 3rd.
ed., (New York: Holt, Rinehart and Winston/ The Dryden Press,
1969), p. 208.

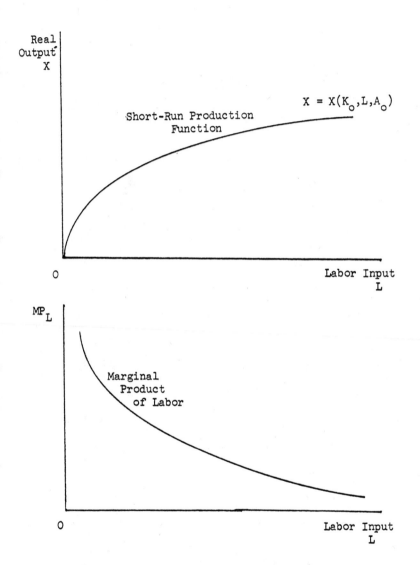

Fig. 1.--The short-run production function and the corresponding marginal product of labor curve.

level with the wage rate divided by the marginal product of labor:

(2.3) $P = W/MP_L$

Using condition (2.3) and assuming the money wage rate fixed
at W_o, the derivation of an aggregate supply curve can be
illustrated in Fig. 2.[6] Quadrant IV gives the short-run production function relating output levels, X, to the labor input, L.
The marginal physical product of labor is drawn in the third
quadrant. By restating equation (2.3) as $W_o = P \cdot MP_L$, the
marginal physical product of labor is related to the price
level in quadrant II. The unitary elastic curve W_o represents
the fixed money wage rate. Finally, in quadrant I, the price
level is related to the level of output. The dotted lines
illustrate the derivation of the aggregate supply curve. At
every point along the aggregate supply curve in quadrant I
labor is being employed to the point where its marginal product
is just equal to the real wage, and firms are maximizing
profits in the short-run. Short-run is stressed in this derivation, since nothing has yet been said about the cost of
utilization of the capital stock.

Before turning attention to capital costs, note that
the aggregate level of employment, output, and the price level
are specified once an aggregate expenditure curve is included.
For example, in Fig. 3, where the aggregate supply curve has

---

[6]Fig. 2. is modified from Keiser, op. cit., p. 303.

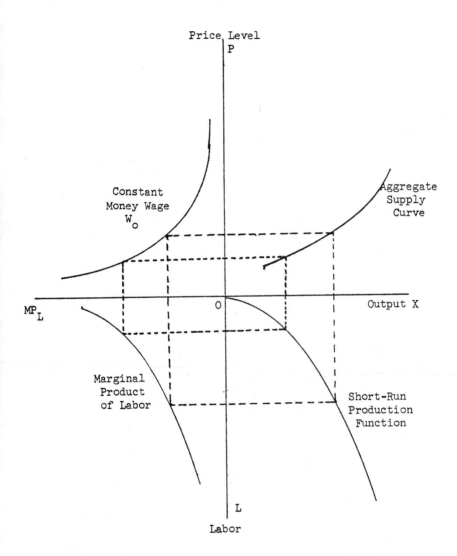

Fig. 2.-- The derivation of the aggregate supply curve.

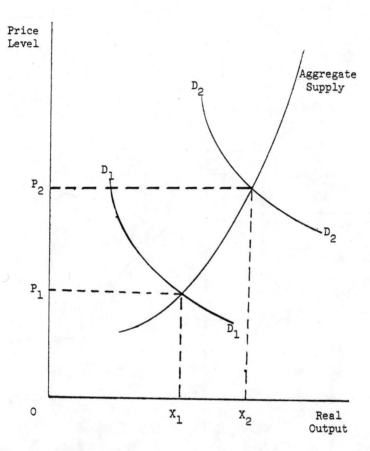

Fig. 3.--The determination of the level of prices and real output.

been reproduced, assume that the total amount of money expenditure on goods and services is given and represented by the curve D_1D_1. By employing the familiar Fisherian equation of exchange, equation (2.4), the rate of aggregate expenditure is represented by

(2.4) $D_1 = MV = PX$

the product of the stock of money, M, times the circular velocity of money.[7] For the moment, a given velocity and a given stock of money are assumed thus resulting in a given, and constant, rate of monetary expenditure. The elasticity of the D_1D_1 curve is, of course, unity. The intersection of the aggregate expenditure curve and the aggregate supply curve jointly determine the actual level of output (and hence employment) and the general price level. If expenditure is proceeding at the rate D_1, the rate of real output will be X_1 and the price level P_1. An increase in aggregate expenditure due to either an increase in the stock of money with velocity constant, or an increase in real demand (increase in V with money held constant), or some combination of both will result in a new, higher, rate of aggregate expenditure, represented by the curve D_2D_2. The result will be an increase in real output to the rate X_2, an increase in employment (provided the economy does not reach

---

[7]For the appropriate index numbers required in an interpretation of the term PX see C. Warburton, "Index Numbers of the Elements of the Equation of Exchange," Depression, Inflation, and Monetary Policy, (Baltimore: Johns Hopkins Press, 1966). An abstract of the above article is found in Econometrica, XVII (April, 1949), p. 176.

full-employment of labor; if it does, the aggregate supply curve becomes vertical), and an increase in the price level to P_2. The increase in the price level is due primarily to the assumption of diminishing returns to labor which, even if the money wage rate remained constant, causes an increase in marginal cost and hence the price at which firms are willing to provide output.

Capital Costs and the Aggregate Supply Curve

The above analysis is deficient in several respects due to the exclusion of any consideration of the place and importance of the capital stock.[8] Entrepreneurs, by supplying real output along the aggregate supply curve, are setting the marginal product of labor equal to the real wage and hence maximizing profits in the short-run. But what precisely is the level of profits? Profits may be maximized and yet be negative. The state of profits will be of major importance in determining whether or not future investment commitments should be undertaken. If an investment function sensitive to short-run profit movements as well as long-run technological considerations is the objective, the cost of capital must be included in the derivation of the aggregate supply curve.

The total cost of production is given simply by the

---

[8]The capital stock is implicitly included when the total product and marginal product of labor curves are drawn, but the position of these curves does not provide sufficient information to determine whether capital is being paid its marginal product.

cost of the factor inputs times the factor inputs employed.
In equation (2.5), W represents the current money wage rate,
R represents the current cost of capital. Since labor is

(2.5) $TC(X) = WL + RK$

measured as a flow variable, there is little conceptual
difficulty in the concept of current wage rate. Capital,
however, is not a flow, but rather a stock of physical assets.
The concept of "current cost"[9] of capital requires further
elaboration. A general interpretation would be simply the
per period cost of maintaining the presence of the capital
input in production. More specifically, current cost is
defined as that cost per period which, when discounted over
the life of the capital good, is just equal to the price of
the capital good. For example, a capital good with an infinite life span will have a price just equal to the infinite
stream of discounted current costs. In equation (2.6), P
represents the price of the capital good, R the current cost,
and r the rate of discount. The value of current cost is

(2.6) $P = \int_0^\infty e^{-rt} R \, dt$

obtained by solving equation (2.6) for R. In this simple
case the current cost is equal to the price of the capital

---

[9]This discussion of the concept of current cost is
based on the analysis presented by Vernon Smith, op. cit.,
(1966), pp. 68-72.

good times the rate of discount.[10] If a capital good with a
finite life span of T years were assumed, equation (2.6)
would become (2.7) and the solution for current cost would

(2.7) $P = \int_0^T e^{-rt} R \, dt$

be, once again, the interest rate times the price of the
capital good times an additional factor taking into account
the depreciation span.[11] Further refinements in the calculation of current cost are possible but will not be pursued here.[12]

In the analysis which follows, it is assumed that entrepreneurs
can calculate the current cost of capital and that this cost is
taken into account when attempting to minimize total current
cost.

The objective of firms is to maximize profit. Money
profits are defined in equation (2.8) as total revenue minus
total costs. Maximizing (2.8) with respect to capital and

(2.8)   Profits = $\pi = P \cdot X(K,L) - WL - RK$

---

[10] Solving for R: $P = R \int_0^\infty e^{-rt} \, dt = \frac{R}{r}(0-1) = R/r$.
Thus, R = rP.

[11] $P = \int_0^T e^{-rt} R \, dt = - \frac{R}{r}(e^{-rT}-1)$. Thus, $R = rP/(1 - e^{-rT})$.
As might be anticipated, the shorter the life span of the
capital good, the higher the current operating cost.

[12] For the computation of current cost when capital
goods are assumed to have a variable life span, see V. Smith,
op. cit., (1966), Chap. VI, "The Theory of Production and
Investment: Capital Goods with Variable Life," pp. 162-184.

labor inputs yields the usual marginal productivity conditions:

(2.9) $\qquad W - u \cdot P \cdot X_L = 0$

(2.10) $\qquad R - u \cdot P \cdot X_K = 0$

The terms X_L and X_K represent the marginal physical products of labor and capital respectively and $\underline{u}$ is the Lagrangean multiplier. Note that equation (2.9) is simply another form of (2.3) which assumed earlier the short-run maximization of profits. By solving (2.1) simultaneously with (2.9) and (2.10), the long-run equilibrium factor inputs are obtained:

(2.11) $\qquad K^* = K^*(W,R,X)$

(2.12) $\qquad L^* = L^*(W,R,X)$

The determination of the optimal factor inputs can be easily illustrated graphically by employing the familiar isoquant diagram. The optimal conditions (2.9) and (2.10) imply that the marginal rate of substitution, X_L/X_K, must equal the negative of the factor price ratio, $-W/R$. For a given rate of final output, say X_0, the optimal factor inputs are those at which the iso-cost curve (in this case, iso-current cost) is just tangent to the isoquant X_0--point A in Fig. 4. If the production function is homogeneous of the first degree, to each rate of output will correspond a unique set of optimal factor inputs. The locus of all these optimal factor combinations is given by the optimal expansion path for the economy, OACE. Note that under the assumption of constant

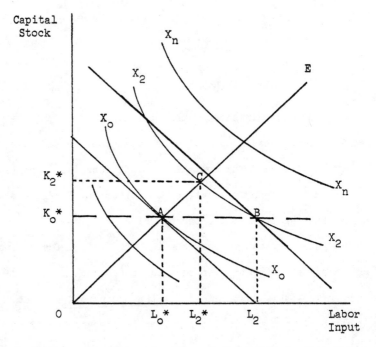

Fig. 4.--The determination of the optimal capital and labor inputs.

returns to scale, whenever the economy attains a point on the
optimal expansion path, the average costs of production for
that rate of production are minimized and, in fact, are equal
to long-run minimum average costs.

Just as   long-run and   short-run production functions
are distinguished, so too the costs of production can be
separated into long-run and short-run functions. Under the
assumption of constant returns to scale, long-run average
costs of production will be constant. However, this is only
in the long-run after the capital stock has adjusted to its
optimal position. In the short-run, with a fixed capital
stock, the cost of production will vary with the level of
output. For example, in Fig. 4, assume that the economy is in
long-run equilibrium producing at a rate of X_o units. If an
increase in aggregate expenditure then occurs, output can
expand simply by hiring more labor inputs (provided that
full-employment of labor has not been encountered). Say
the new production rate is X_2 units with a labor input of L_2
and the given capital stock of K_o^*. At point B, labor is
being paid its marginal product, but capital is not optimally
adjusted. The optimal capital input is at point C which can
be attained only through the process of investment increasing
the capital stock to K_2^*. The short-run total cost function
would be represented by equation (2.13) where K_o represents

(2.13) $TC(X) = WL(X) + RK_o$

the existing stock of capital. The labor input is, of course,

a function of the rate of final output. The average cost
function in the short-run will also depend only on the rate
of final output:

(2.14) $\quad AC(X) = \dfrac{WL(X)}{X} + \dfrac{RK_0}{X}$

Both the long-run and short-run cost functions are
illustrated in Fig. 5. The long-run average cost curve is
derived under the assumption that both capital and labor are
optimally adjusted. Therefore, when the average cost curve
reaches its minimum level, that rate of output represents
the optimal rate of output for the given stock of capital.
The optimal rate of output is defined as that rate of output
which, given the current price ratios of factor inputs and
the current state of technology, minimizes the average costs
of production. As the capital stock increases, the rate of
output which is "optimal" will also increase. This is simply
the long-run relationship between capital and output illustrated by the equilibrium expansion path of Fig. 4., p. 34.
This relationship has been transferred to the capital-output
plane in Fig. 5 where it is represented by the line $X = \dfrac{1}{v}K$.
The parameter v, which has been referred to as the capital-
output ratio, is not a constant. Rather, it is a function of
factor prices in the economy and the current state of technology.
If, in addition, the production function is subject to noncon-
stant returns to scale, it will also be a function of the
rate of output.

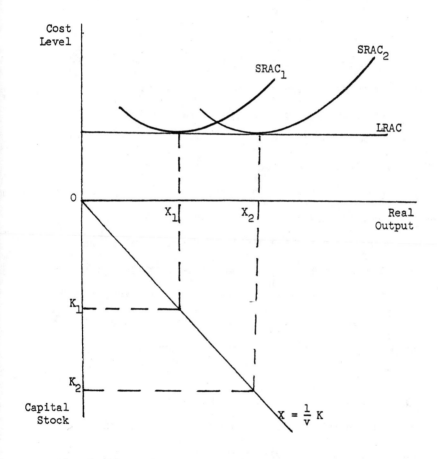

Fig. 5.--The relationship between the capital stock and the optimal rate of output and the corresponding cost curves.

Capital and the Optimal Rate of Output

Before examining further the implications of changing factor prices or technology for the capital-output ratio, v, the aggregate supply curve derived earlier is combined with the average cost of production curve. In Fig. 6, an aggregate supply curve and the corresponding average cost of production curve have been drawn for two separate capital stocks. If the initial rate of aggregate expenditure is given by D_1, which intersects the aggregate supply curve at point A, the economy will be in equilibrium with the price level P_0 and the rate of real output X_0. For the given stock of capital, the rate of output at point A will be optimal in that capital is being used most efficiently. Labor, also, is being used efficiently in that labor is being paid its marginal product. However, full-employment of the labor force is not assumed. In fact, if there is to be any subsequent increase in output due to an increase in expenditure, some level of unemployment must exist. This is consistent with the assumption of a fixed money wage rate.

If the rate of expenditure should increase from D_1 to D_2, the short-run impact will be an increase in the price level to P_1 and an increase in real output to X_1. Under the assumed conditions, at a rate of output of X_1, labor is still being paid its marginal product, but capital is now in short supply. As a result, firms in the economy are earning a pure profit represented by the area $EBCP_1$. Note that while the average

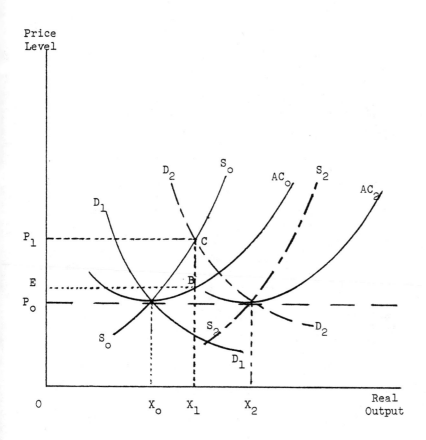

Fig. 6.--The determination of prices and output under short-run movements in aggregate demand and long-run adjustments in the capital stock.

cost of production has increased by the increase in output
from X_o units per period to X_1 units, the price level has
increased considerably more. The aggregate price level is
set to cover the marginal cost of production, which, of
course, will exceed the average cost. The resulting situation is a state of disequilibrium which has an
 inherent   tendency to correct itself. At a production rate
of X_1 units; the capital stock is insufficient, i.e. less than
optimal, capital is earning a return greater than "normal."
An incentive to increase the capital stock exists on two
counts. One is that average costs would be reduced by expanding
the capital stock which, if all prices remained constant, would
in itself further increase profits. The second factor is that
the availability of profits above the "normal" rate of return
provides additional funds with which to finance new investment.[13]
As the capital stock is expanded, the average cost curve will
gradually shift to the right. With no change in the rate of
aggregate expenditure, the rate of output would eventually
settle at X_2 units; a point where again there are no profits
being earned in the economy and both capital and labor are being
paid their marginal products.

So far the current cost of capital and the current money
wage rate have been assumed constant. Allowing them to vary

---

[13]The relationship between profits and the financing of
investment expenditures is discussed below in Chapter IV.

introduces few complications. If, in the process of expansion, the money wage rate should rise due to conditions on the labor market, the current stock of capital would become optimal for a smaller rate of output. The aggregate supply curve would shift to the left. Similarly, an increase in the operating cost of capital would cause the supply curve to shift to the right.

To provide a concrete example, assume that the aggregate production function in the economy can be represented by a Cobb-Douglas production function, equation (2.16). The

$$(2.16) \qquad X = AK^{\alpha}L^{\beta}$$

expansion path is specified in (2.17). To obtain an expression

$$(2.17) \qquad R/W = (\alpha L)/(\beta K)$$

for the optimal capital input as a function of the rate of output, solve equation (2.17) for K and substitute this value into (2.16) The result, equation (2.18), gives an expression for the optimal labor input. Replacing L in (2.17) with L* and

$$(2.18) \qquad L* = \frac{X}{A}(W\alpha/R\beta)^{-\alpha}$$

solving yields the optimal capital input as a function of factor costs, technology, and output. The capital-optimal output ratio, $\underline{v}$,

$$(2.19) \qquad K* = \frac{X}{A}(\frac{W}{R}\frac{\alpha}{\beta})^{\beta}$$

can now be defined explicitly for a Cobb-Douglas world:

$$(2.20) \qquad v = v(W,R,A,\alpha,\beta) = (\frac{W\alpha}{R\beta})^{\beta}\frac{1}{A}$$

With equation (2.20) it is possible to state explicitly the effect of a change in factor prices or in technology, represented by the parameters A, α, and β, on the relationship between the existing stock of capital and the rate of output considered optimal for that existing stock. An increase in the money wage rate or the elasticity of output with respect to capital will increase the capital-output ratio, or, what is the same thing, with the existing stock of capital the rate of output for which it is optimal expands. Similarly, an increase in the current cost of capital, the elasticity of output with respect to labor, or the rate of technical change, A, will decrease the capital-optimal output ratio. The supply curve will shift to the left and the existing stock of capital will become optimal for a smaller rate of real output. These comparative static results are summarized below:

(2.21) $\qquad \dfrac{\delta v}{\delta W} > 0, \quad \dfrac{\delta v}{\delta \alpha} > 0, \quad \dfrac{\delta v}{\delta R} < 0, \quad \dfrac{\delta v}{\delta \beta} < 0, \quad \dfrac{\delta v}{\delta A} < 0$

Chapter III

AGGREGATE DEMAND AND THE CONSUMPTION FUNCTION

The Concept of Aggregate Demand

Few areas of economics have advanced as far and have
gained as much acceptance as that of the theory of demand.
Given very general assumptions on utility-maximizing consumers,
individual demand curves relating price and quantity demanded
are constructed. These then are aggregated to derive aggregate demand curves for particular industries. It would seem,
at first glance, a natural extension to aggregate industry
curves and derive an "aggregate demand curve" for the economy;
but it is not.[1] For any single product, demand curves are
derived on the assumption of ceteris paribus, all other things
equal. When attempting to formulate an aggregate demand
curve for final output, however, all other things are decidedly
not equal. Individual or industry demand curves relate the
price of a commodity to the quantities desired. On the aggregate basis, it is not clear either what price is appropriate[2]
or what the exact relationship between price and output changes

_____

[1]For a discussion of some of the problems inherent in
macroanalysis see F. Brooman and N. Jacoby, Macroeconomics:
An Introduction to Theory and Policy (Chicago: Aldine Publishing Co., 1970), pp. 1-9.

[2]e.g. wholesale price index, consumer price index, or
GNP deflator.

is or, for that matter, whether aggregate demand should be defined in terms of price at all.

The precise meaning of "aggregate demand" seems to vary considerably from author to author. Keynes originally defined an "aggregate demand function" which related the level of expenditures in an economy to the level of employment.[3] Although this definition has been adopted by others,[4] it is not universally used. A closely related definition to that of Keynes' defines an aggregate demand function as a relationship between total expenditure and the level of real income.[5] Neither of these definitions relates the price level explicitly to the rate of real output, although other writers have defined aggregate demand curves in this manner.[6] Aggregate demand curves relating price and output have generally taken two forms: one a simple rectangular hyperbola indicating a level of money expenditure,[7] the other a downward sloping function relating

_____

[3] J. M. Keynes, The General Theory of Employment, Interest and Money, (New York: Harcourt, Brace & World, Inc, 1964), p. 25.

[4] See, for example, S. Weintraub, An Approach to the Theory of Income Distribution (Philadelphia: Chilton, 1958) and P. Davidson and E. Smolensky, Aggregate Supply and Demand Analysis (New York: Harper & Row, Publishers, 1964).

[5] Brooman and Jacoby, op. cit., p. 238.

[6] Lindauer defines an aggregate demand curve as depicting "the total amount of commodities that would be purchased in an economy at each level of commodity prices." J. Lindauer, Macroeconomics (New York: John Wiley & Sons, 1968), p. 184.

[7] This approach is used by N. F. Keiser, Macroeconomics (New York: Random House, 1971), pp. 304-06, and E. Shapiro,

price levels to real output.

A number of reasons have been postulated to justify the inverse relationship between price and output indicated by the downward sloping aggregate demand concept. A rise in the price level reduces the real supply of money which, in turn, increases interest rates and thus reduces real aggregate demand.[8] An increase in the price level will also have the effect of reducing the real value of the financial assets of the community and depressing the level of real demand. This is the "Pigou-effect."[9] Other possible influences include the effects of a progressive tax structure,[10] the net foreign investment effect,[11] and any effects of a redistribution of income subsequent to price level changes.[12]

This particular form of an aggregate demand curve has

Macroeconomic Analysis , second edition (New York: Harcourt, Brace & World, Inc., 1970), pp. 323-327.

[8]This is the only influence Keynes was able to find relating the price level to real output. Keynes,op. cit.,pp.257-79.

[9]A.C.Pigou, "The Classical Stationary State," Economic Journal, LIII (1943), pp. 343-351.

[10]With a given real income, money incomes rise with the price level. A progressive tax structure will increase tax receipts relative to real disposable income. This effect, of course, can be nullified by increased government spending or a reduction of tax rates.

[11]An increase in the price level relative to that of other countries will tend to increase imports and decrease exports.

[12]See G.L.Bach and A. Ando, "The Redistributional Effects of Inflation,"Review of Economics and Statistics,XXXIX (February, 1957), pp. 1-13.

been derived graphically[13] by assuming any given fixed price
level and then examining the resulting equilibrium level of
real income as determined by the intersection of the IS and
LM curves.[14] This price-income combination determines one
point on the "aggregate demand curve." By assuming a different
price level, either the IS or LM or both relationships will
shift, indicating a new level of equilibrium income and a new
price-income combination for the aggregate demand curve. By
repeating this process, the entire aggregate demand curve is
derived, every point of which represents an equilibrium level
of real income.

The usefulness of an "aggregate demand curve" defined
in this manner is subject to serious question. If one were
interested only in equilibrium positions, then the intersection of the aggregate demand curve and the aggregate
supply curve would determine jointly a real income level and
a general price level at which the money market, the commodity
market, and the labor market are in equilibrium, and by
equilibrium in the labor market all that is meant in this
context is that labor is being paid its marginal product.

---

[13]Lindauer, op. cit., pp.191-93 and J. McKenna, Aggregate
Economic Analysis (New York:Holt, Rinehart and Winston/The
Dryden Press, 1969), p.198.

[14]J. R. Hicks, "Mr. Keynes and the 'Classics':A Suggested
Interpretation," Econometrica, V (April, 1937), reprinted in
W. Fellner and B. F. Haley (eds.), Readings in the Theory of Income
Distribution (Philadelphia: Blakiston Co., 1946), pp.461-76.

But this resulting "equilibrium" is perhaps a misnomer. Not
only might there be large numbers of unemployed workers in
the economy, with this formulation nothing at all is known
about the state of the capital market. The rate of return
to capital may or may not be equal to its marginal physical
product. If it is not, one could hardly call this an equilibrium position.

A more serious objection is that this approach yields
no indication of what in fact does determine the real output
and price level in any given period. If real output is not
at the equilibrium level, it must be at some other level and
the price that accompanies the actual real income is indeter-
minant in this framework. Few economies are ever in equilibrium
in either the commodity or the money markets. A demand curve
based on the assumption of equilibrium will, therefore, be
of no use if an explanation is sought for the determination
of the actual rate of real output and the actual price level.

Yet another definition of "aggregate demand curve" is
available in the literature. If the total amount of money
expenditure can be assumed given, then this money expenditure
can result in any one of a number of different real output
levels depending on the prevailing price level. The given
level of money expenditure can be represented in the price-
output plane by a rectangular hyperbola. The elasticity of
such an "aggregate demand curve" is, of course, unity. This

definition has been employed by Normal Keiser[15] and by E. Shapior.[16]
These authors, however, have also insisted on incorporating a
concept of equilibrium into their aggregate demand curve.
Keiser merely asserts the fact of equilibrium: "Each demand
curve is an equilibrium one in which $C + I + G_p + (X-M)$ is equal
to income (or supply)."[17] Shapiro attempts a graphical derivation, but his proceedure is open to some question since he
translates, in the process, conclusions obtained from the
real analysis to conclusions appropriate in monetary terms.[18]
If real consumption depends on real income at constant prices,
it does not follow that money consumption will depend on money
income at variable prices.

Objections to the use of an equilibrium concept in
aggregate demand are as valid for this approach as for the one
discussed previously. Indeed, it is not clear why it is necessary
to assume that any given level of expenditures represents an
equilibrium level before the price level and the real output
rate can be determined. In fact, the level of expenditures in
an economy at any given moment is more likley to be a disequili-

---

[15]Keiser, op. cit.,pp.304-6. [16]Shapiro, op. cit.,pp.323-7

[17]Keiser, op. cit., p. 304.

[18]"In the earlier discussion, we described each aggregate demand function as showing how aggregate real expenditures
would vary with real income, for there we assumed that the price
level remained unchanged in the face of shifts in the aggregate
demand function. Since we have now dropped that assumption,
the aggregate demand function is expressed here in money terms
and shows how aggregate money expenditures will vary with the
money value of income." Shapiro, op. cit., p. 324.

brium level as the economy is attempting to adjust its real
and monetary forces toward an equilibrium position which itself
is constantly changing through time. In the analysis which
follows, aggregate monetary expenditures will be viewed in
this light. Aggregate real demand will be a function of real
components of the macroeconomic system. The translation, then,
of this real demand into monetary expenditure will depend upon
the money stock and the actions of the authorities controlling
the money stock, as well as the current price level or the
price level expected to prevail during the period. Whether
or not the real demand will be realized depends on supply
conditions within the economy.

The Consumption Function

Since Keynes' original formulation, the consumption
function has been the subject of considerable economic debate
and empirical investigation.[19] Keynes believed that the primary
determinant of consumption expenditures was income. Subsequent
research has upheld this contention, although the precise
nature of the dependence remains in question. The definition
of consumption function, itself, should be considered with some
care. A distinction should be made between a theoretical

---

[19] For a review of studies of consumption see R. Ferber,
"Research on Household Behavior," American Economic Review, LII
(March, 1962), pp.19-55; D. Suits, "The Determinants of Consumer
Expenditure: A Review of Present Knowledge," in Commission on
Money and Credit, Impacts of Monetary Policy (Englewood Cliffs,
N.J.: Prentice-Hall, 1963), pp. 1-57.

consumption function and an empirical consumption function.
Empirical consumption functions have been estimated by linear
regression techniques relating various measures of income to
consumption.[20] These estimates do not necessarily define a
consumption function for much the same reason that plotting
price and quantity indices over time may define neither a demand
function nor a supply function.[21] Observed consumption expenditures at varying income levels indicate only the consumption
actually achieved and not necessarily the consumption "desired"
at the corresponding income levels. As a consequence, empirical
consumption functions tell us only the mean rate of consumption
expenditure actually obtained with given income flows.

The theoretical consumption function, on the other hand,
can be viewed in two respects. One would relate real consumption expenditures desired to real income levels. Thus, at
any given income level, the consumption function would state
the amount of real consumption desired. Another interpretation
would be that actual real consumption obtained in any period
is a function of actual real income experienced in that period.
This would represent a theoretical relationship and the empirical

---

[20]Numerous examples of empirical consumption functions
are presented in Keiser, op. cit., pp.79-118, and in M.K.Evans
Macroeconomic Activity: Theory, Forecasting, and Control
(New York: Harper and Row, 1969), pp. 150-172.

[21]This is part of the "identification problem" in econometrics. For a discussion see L.R.Klein, An Introduction to
Econometrics (Englewood Cliffs, N.J.: Prentice-Hall, Inc.,
1962), pp. 8-18.

consumption functions would be estimates of the "true" relation.
This interpretation is, perhaps, somewhat better than the former.
Human nature being what it is, everyone probably demands in
real terms considerably more than his income would allow. Man
is seldom satiated in goods and services. However, actual
expenditures are always limited to some extent by current income. Therefore, the consumption function might best be expressed as the relationship between real consumption expenditure
and real income.

The analysis of aggregate consumption has often proceeded
on the basis of only the real variables in the system. Prices
and money are abstracted from and assumed not to effect demand
conditions. This is unfortunate since the inclusion of prices
does not preclude the analysis of price effects which may in
some instances have very important effects.[22] The concentration
on real variables has also tended to obscure the fact that
what is being considered are flow variables and not stocks.
Income is expressed as a flow of money payments. This flow
of money payments is then converted into a flow of money

---

[22]B. Ohlin has noted the advantages of dealing in
monetary rather than strictly real terms. He argued, "A
reasoning in monetary terms does not prevent any amount of
considerations of the 'real' implications, whenever such
considerations may be desirable, e.g., in a discussion of
policy. But it has the advantage of permitting a much simpler
and less sophisticated explanation of the market phenomena,
which are price phenomena." B. Ohlin, "Some Notes on the
Stockholm Theory of Saving and Investments II," Economic
Journal, XLVII (1937), p. 230.

expenditure, a flow of dollars in exchange for real goods.

Both the Classical and Keynesian analysis of aggregates can be expressed in terms of these money flows. In the Classical system[23] the flow of aggregate expenditure was not regarded as a serious problem. All money income flowing into the household sector flowed out of the household sector either in the form of consumption expenditure or in the form of savings. Savings were possible only by either accumulating money stocks or financial assets. Since money in itself yielded no return whereas financial assets did, it was assumed that savings would predominantly be directed into financial assets. The key variable in deciding precisely what the proportions between consumption expenditure and savings would be was the interest rate. An increase in interest rates would result in a larger proportion of money income being directed into savings. A decrease in interest rates would produce the opposite result. Investment expenditures of firms were financed by savings within the system. Investment expenditures depended on the rate of interest: a decrease in interest rates would increase the rate of investment, an increase would slow down investment expenditures. The interest rate, then, played the primary role in insuring that the total   income flowing to households would eventually be directed into the purchase of final

---

[23]For an extensive discussion of Classical macroeconomics see G. Ackley, Macroeconomic Theory (New York: The Macmillan Co., 1961), Chaps. V-VIII, pp. 105-167.

products. The only effect of an introduction of a larger
stock of money into the system would be an increase in the
aggregate price level. Since the Classical system assumed
flexibility of wages and prices, the labor market would be
continually at the full-employment level and hence output
would be at its maximum rate. An increase in expenditure
could not bring forth an increase in real output, hence
prices had to rise.

In the Keynesian system, the key variable in deciding
the division between consumption and saving was not the interest
rate but rather the rate of income flow. As money incomes increased, more money would be directed into consumption expenditure, but the proportion of income directed into consumption
would decrease. If the money expenditures desired by businesses
for investment fell short of the savings supplied, there was no
longer any automatic adjustment mechanism to insure that the
flow of savings would decrease to match the decreased demand
for investment. It was now possible that the total amount of
money income received would not all be directed back into a
corresponding amount of money expenditure.

There are two key questions which must be considered:
one, what precisely does determine the division of money income
into consumption expenditure and saving, and two, if total money
income is not directed back entirely into total aggregate expenditure, where is it directed? This latter question will be
considered when the effects of monetary changes are examined.

Empirical estimates of the consumption function have yielded two separate estimates of the relationship between consumption and income. If a short-run function is estimated, one obtains a marginal propensity to consume less than one and a falling average propensity to consume. However, estimates of the long-run relationship between consumption and income have implied a constant average propensity to consume equal to the marginal propensity to consume. This same relationship can be obtained by examining only periods of relatively full-employment. Periods which include cyclical fluctuations, on the other hand, correspond to the short-run relation.

A number of explanations have been offered to explain the conflicting long-run and short-run results. One of the earliest was that the consumption function was basically non-proportional and that the long-run results were obtained purely by coincidence as the short-run function was continually shifting upward through time.[24] Several reasons were advanced for an upward shifting consumption function including an increasing population, changes in age distribution, and the constant introduction of new commodities. James Duesenberry attempted to explain the difference by asserting that consumption depended not only on current income but also on previous peak income.[25]

---

[24]A. Smithies, "Forecasting Postwar Demand: I," Econometrica, XIII (January, 1945).

[25]J. Duesenberry, Income, Saving, and the Theory of Consumer Behavior(Cambridge:Harvard University, 1952).

Milton Friedman's explanation was given in terms of "permanent income" and "permanent consumption" concepts.[26]

The consumption function assumed in this study is based on yet another attempted reconciliation called the life-cycle hypothesis.[27] By assuming utility-maximizing consumers who base consumption decisions on the present value of the total resources expected over the consumer's life span, an aggregate consumption function is derived which relates consumption expenditures to current income and to aggregate net worth in the economy. In a very simplified economy net worth is represented by the net accumulated savings of all the individuals in the economy. Individuals accumulate savings by increasing their cash balances or by purchasing financial assets. The financial assets may be purchased from firms as new securities or existing financial assets may be purchased from other consumers. The rationale for saving depends on a number of factors, one of the most important of which is the desire to consume. Many commodities desired by consumers, such as houses and durable goods, require cash payments in excess of the money available from current income flows. The only way to make these purchases is by the accumulation of savings.

---

[26]M. Friedman, A Theory of the Consumption Function (Princeton: Princeton University Press, 1957).

[27]A. Ando and F. Modigliani, "The 'Life Cycle' Hypothesis of Saving: Aggregate Implications and Tests," American Economic Review, LIII (March, 1963), pp. 55-84; reprinted in A. Zellner, ed., Readings in Economic Statistics and Econometrics (Boston: Little, Brown and Co., 1968), pp. 290-319. A bibliography of earlier work on the 'Life Cycle' hypothesis is provided here.

When sufficient savings have been obtained, the consumption
expenditure can take place. Therefore, while some consumers
are attempting to build up their net worth by saving, others
may be in the process of consuming their accumulated net worth
by drawing down their financial balances. Some consumers will
be directing more than their current money income into consumption while others are directing less than their current money
income into consumption. It is clear, therefore, that the only
way the net financial assets of the economy can be increased
is through an increase in the stock of money or by an increase
in the amount of financial securities.

For purposes of simplicity, assume that the only kind of
security is represented by a bond. The life of the bond is
approximately equal to the anticipated life of the capital
goods in the economy. Bonds are issued by firms for the purpose
of securing money balances. These money balances are then used
to finance the accumulation of capital assets. As a result,
the amount of bonds outstanding in the economy will be proportional to the capital stock. Increases in the capital stock will
not only increase the output-producing capacity of the economy,
but also serve to increase the net worth, and hence shift the
consumption function upward. Equation (3.1) gives the amount

(3.1) $$C_t = C_t(X_t, M_t, B_t) = c_o X_t + c_1(M_t + B_t)$$

of real consumption, C_t, in time period $\underline{t}$ as a function of
real output and the accumulated net worth of the economy represented by the total money balances, M_t, and real bonds, B_t.

As a first approximation, assume that the consumption function
is linear and the net worth is represented simply by the sum of
current real money and bond stocks. The parameters c_o and c_1 are
assumed constant. To the extent that consumers desire a particular
arrangement in their portfolio between money and bonds, each may
have a separate effect on consumption. However, for simplicity,
assume that money is accumulated only for the purposes of trans-
actions and that any net saving is accomplished by the purchase
of bonds. Since the stock of bonds outstanding is proportional
to the stock of capital, the real consumption function can be
rewritten as a function of real output and the capital stock:

$$(3.2) \qquad C_t = C_t(X_t, K_t) = c_o X_t + c_2 K_t$$

Real Demand, Monetary Demand, and the Price Level

To translate the real consumption function into monetary
expenditure some assumption must be made about price expectations.
The simplest is that consumers expect the current price level to
continue into the future. Thus if C_t represents the real consumption demand in period $\underline{t}$, the amount of monetary expenditure
needed to fulfill this real demand is given by equation (3.3)
where c_t is consumption expenditure and P_{t-1} is the price level

$$(3.3) \qquad c_t = P_{t-1} C_t$$

in the preceeding period. Note that if the total amount of real
demand exceeds that of the previous period, even if prices remain
constant the expenditure necessary to obtain it must exceed the
total monetary expenditure received in the preceeding period.

Therefore, the only way that consumers could, in fact, attain the necessary monetary expenditure would be to increase the velocity of the given stock of money or to obtain the necessary additional funds from the banking system. Velocity, of course, is not a given constant and can fluctuate somewhat in the short-run. However, to avoid for the moment the complications of a changing velocity, assume that any additional money required to realize the real demand is supplied by the banking system.

The determinants of real investment demand will be discussed in Chapter IV. At this stage, simply assume that firms have decided what rate of real investment they would like to maintain and hence the money expenditure required and denote this rate by i_t. Total expenditure in the given period is then represented by the sum of consumption expenditure and investment expenditure. This sum is denoted by $D_t = c_t + i_t$ (necessarily also equal to $M_t V_t$) and is illustrated in Fig. 7 by the rectangular hyperbolas D_o, D_1, or D_2.

Fig. 7 can be used to illustrate the relationship between movements in real demand, monetary demand, and the capital stock. Assume that the economy is in an initial state of equilibrium represented by point A. With the given stock of capital the optimal rate of output is X_o and the supply curve is given by S_o. If the rate of aggregate expenditure in the initial period happens to be D_o, then the economy will be in a state of equilibrium in which factors are being paid their marginal products and output is being produced at the lowest possible cost. If,

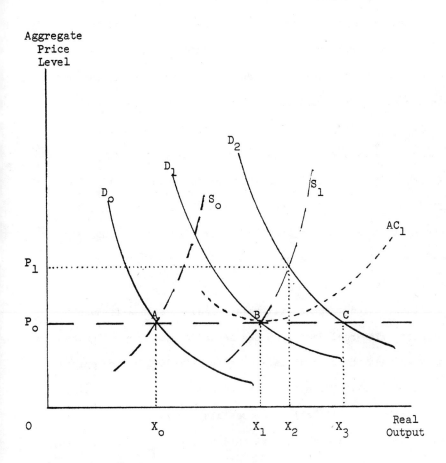

Fig. 7.--The relationship between demand and supply shifts, prices, and the rate of output.

in the following period, the sum of real consumption demand and
real investment demand is represented by a rate of output equal
to X_1, then aggregate monetary expenditure will be given by
the aggregate demand curve D_1. Real investment expenditures,
provided they are sufficient to replace that part of the capital
stock subject to depreciation, will maintain or increase the
existing stock of capital. If the existing stock of capital
is increased sufficiently to move the optimal rate of output
to X_1, the aggregate supply curve in the following period will
shift from S_0 to S_1. The average cost of production with the
new capital stock is given by AC_1. Under these conditions,
the economy will once more be in a state of equilibrium at
point B similar to that at point A.

In practice, events will seldom lead to such a fortunate
occurrence. The real demand in the second period may be larger
or smaller than the optimal rate of output implied by the existing capital stock. But even if the economy is not at an equilibrium position, it will still be possible to determine the
actual price level and the actual rate of output. To illustrate,
suppose real demand desired in the next period were X_3 rather than
X_1. The rate of monetary expenditure consumers believe necessary
to obtain this real output is given by the aggregate demand
curve D_2. The capital stock, however, is only sufficient to
produce the rate of output X_1 at maximum efficiency. Output
rates exceeding X_1 can only be produced at a higher level of
prices. The short-run result is indicated by the point D in Fig. 7.

Real output is increased, but so   is the price level. The
actual rate of output would be X_2 while the price level would
rise to P_1. Unlike the Keynesian model where increases in
money demand lead to the desired increases in real output or
the Classical system where increases in money demand result
only in higher prices, the present model indicates a result
much closer to reality. When an economy is operating at or
near full capacity, increases in demand are likely to be met
by a simultaneous increase in prices and output.

The present discussion has assumed that investment
rates have been determined and are given. It now remains
to focus attention on the determinants of real investment
demand. This is the problem tackled in Chapter IV.

Chapter IV

THE DETERMINANTS OF AGGREGATE INVESTMENT

Adjustment From Disequilibrium

Unless the current rate of output is the optimal rate,
that is, a rate at which both capital and labor are earning their
marginal products, the economy will be in a state of disequilibrium.
There are a number of ways in which this disequilibrium can be
corrected. In Fig. 8, assume that an initial equilibrium had
been attained at point A with a rate of output X_o and the aggregate price level just equal to long-run average cost. If the
rate of aggregate demand, D_o, is increased to D_1, the rate of
output will expand to X_1 and the price level increase to P_1.
These magnitudes are determined by the intersection of the aggregate demand and aggregate supply curves at point B. At the given
factor prices, the stock of capital appropriate to the new,
higher, rate of output is K_1. The disequilibrium could be eliminated by an expansion of the current stock of capital towards its
new equilibrium level. However, it need not be assumed that this
is the only way in which the current disequilibrium situation
would correct itself. It is quite reasonable to suppose that
some of the adjustment would be felt in the factor markets. For
example, the higher rate of output will lead to a desire on the
part of firms to expand their current rate of investment. But if
the monetary authorities do not expand the current stock of

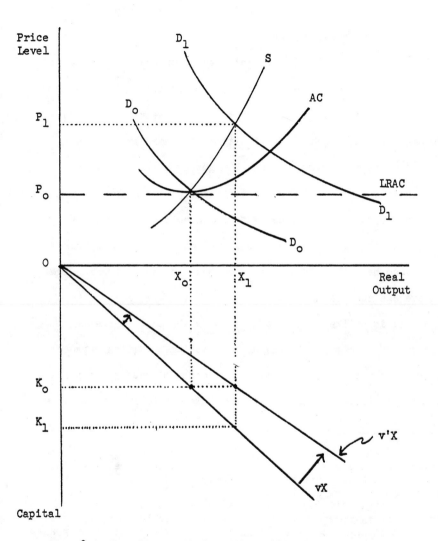

Fig. 8.--The adjustment from disequilibrium.

money and consumers do not suddenly increase their rate of
savings, there will be no expansion in the funds available for
investment. The increase in the demand for investment funds
without a corresponding increase in supply will lead to a rise
in the interest rate. As interest rates increase, the relationship between the stock of capital and the optimal rate of output
is changed; the line vX in Fig. 8 shifts to the right. If
consumers and the monetary authorities are unaffected by the
rising interest rates, the line vX might eventually shift to
the line v'X where the current stock of capital is now the
appropriate stock for the new rate of output. With no other
changes in the system except the increased capital cost, this
would also have the effect over the long-run of raising the long-
run average cost of production.[1]

It is unlikely that conditions in the labor market would
lead to any correction in the disequilibrium condition represented by the point B. The short-run expansion of output was possible
only by the hiring of more workers. This, of course, implicitly

---

[1]It should be born in mind that the static analysis being
employed at this stage is used merely to indicate the direction
in which the major variables are likely to move. An immediate
adjustment to a new equilibrium position would not be expected
within a single time period. And with each new period, the position of the aggregate supply curve will itself be changing as will
be the position of aggregate demand. Thus, the equilibrium position the economy is seeking will be changing from period to period.
A continuous state of equilibrium in the economy would require a
state of growth in which producers in each period correctly anticipated the increase in aggregate demand and provided precisely
that capital stock needed. The growth of the system will be
discussed below in Chapter V.

assumes a condition of unemployment. If any changes at all
occur in the current money wage rate, they are likely to be in
the direction of increasing money wages. The effect of an
increase in money wage rates would be to rotate the optimal
capital-output line to the left which would only increase the
degree of disequilibrium and increase the desirability of increasing investment expenditures.

In reality, what is most likely to happen in any economy
is a simultaneous adjustment of both factor prices and the rate
of investment. Since focus here, however, centers on capital
adjustment, the effects of factor price changes will be placed
in a subsidiary role. Attention is concentrated on adjustments
in the capital stock as the vehicle eliminating disequilibrium.

The Reaction of the Individual Firm

Before considering the macroeconomic adjustments in the
capital stock, it would be useful at this juncture to examine
briefly the position of the individual firm. Since prices are
beyond the control of individual firms (recall this is an economy
of perfect competition), the expansion in aggregate expenditure
is experienced simply as a higher price for their products, and,
of course, an increase in profits. Fig. 9. illustrates the
position of the individual firm. Originally in a state of equilibrium producing x_o units at a price of p_o, the firm will expand
output to x_1 when the price rises to p_1, or perhaps more accurately,
the firm will sell the additional units demanded only at the price
of p_1. Profits are represented by the area $ABCP_1$. The firm is

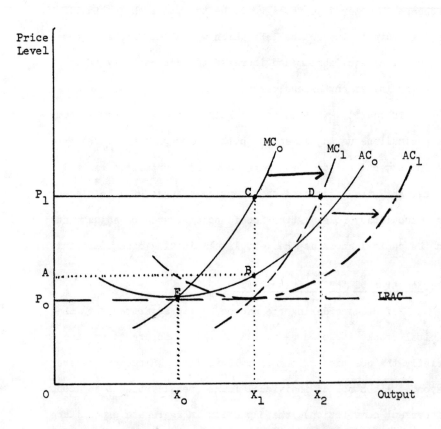

Fig. 9.--Microeconomic adjustments of the individual firm.

not, however, in a long-run equilibrium position; average cost
of production exceeds long-run average cost. There will be an
incentive for each firm to increase its capital stock by increasing
its current rate of investment. As the firm increases its capital
stock, its average cost curve (and its supply curve) shift to
the right. For example, in Fig. 9 average cost might shift from
AC_o to AC_1. The rate of output would increase to x_2 units. The
firm would experience another increase in profits if the price
level remained steady at p_1. Of course, with all firms under an
inducement to expand capacity, the aggregate supply curve will
also be shifting to the right as the capital stock expands and
if aggregate expenditure remains steady, the price level will
itself fall until the combined effect of increasing aggregate
supply and constant aggregate expenditure move the aggregate
price level back to its long-run minimum level, thus eliminating
any abnormal profits in the economy.

The conclusions for an individual firm are readily extended to the entire economy. An increase in money expenditure will
lead, in the short-run, to an increase in both output and prices.
At the new higher rate of output, the capital stock is no longer
at its optimum level and capital adjustment is called for. An
increase in the rate of investment will increase the given capital
stock, shifting the aggregate supply curve to the right and increasing the optimum rate of output. This process of expansion
will continue until the long-run equilibrium price and output appropriate to the increased money expenditure are obtained.

The Potential Profitability of Capital Stock Adjustment

The inducement to invest can be illustrated by two factors, both of which reflect the same phenomenon. On the one hand, the increased expenditure leads to an increase in profits, which in itself will facilitate increased investment. The profits are, originally, acquired by the owners of capital, implying that the actual return to physical capital exceeds the current cost of capital. This occurs because for the given interest and wage structure, the current rate of output exceeds the optimum rate for the given stock of capital. Another way of looking at the same thing is to point out that the average cost of production is above the long-run minimum cost because the capital stock is deficient. The magnitude of the profits being earned or of the difference between current average cost and long-run minimum average cost is reflected in the degree to which the current rate of output exceeds the optimal. The higher the current rate above the optimal, the stronger is the inducement to invest. Firms will invest in capital because it is profitable, or potentially profitable, to do so. It is this profit motive of investment which determines the rate at which the stock of capital in an economy will grow.

Fig. 10 illustrates the relationship between the profitability of capital expansion and the rate of output. Assume an economy initially in equilibrium at point A with aggregate expenditure given by D_o and the capital stock given at K_o. Price and output are P_o and X_o respectively. Now assume that, for some

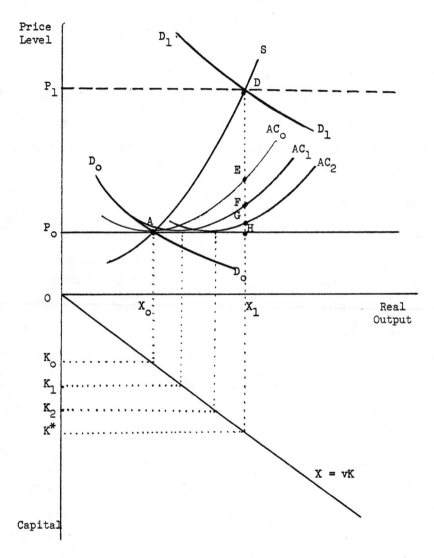

Fig. 10.--The relationship between the profitability of capital expansion and the rate of real output.

reason, the rate of aggregate expenditure increases to D_1. In the short-run, output will increase to X_1 and the price level rise to P_1. Originally, the average cost curve is represented by AC_o and ,hence, average profit is given by the distance DE. To examine the consequence of investment, imagine three successive increases in capital, each of equal magnitude. The first increase in investment shifts the average cost curve to AC_1. If the price level were to remain unchanged, average profit would be increased by the amount EF, the reduction in cost for the rate of output X_1. Another unit increment in the capital stock would again reduce average cost, although by not as much as did the first increment. Average profit is now represented by DG. Another increment in capital would bring the capital stock to the optimum level, K*, but the additional reduction in cost would be relatively minor, represented in Fig. 10 by the distance GH.

It is clear that as the capital stock increases toward its optimal level, the inducement to investment decreases in intensity. That is, when the actual rate of output is close to the optimal rate although it exceeds it, the degree to which capital is over-utilized is relatively minor and the return to capital over its marginal product also quite minor. On the other hand, when aggregate demand is such that the capital stock is considerably deficient, there will be a much stronger inducement to invest because the profits to be earned by so doing are far greater. This relationship between capital and profits, or rather between capital and potential profits, is given in Fig. 11. The initial stock of

capital is K_o. A change in demand conditions or, in fact, in any
parameter which determines the desired stock of capital, has
changed the desired stock from its present level to K*. With a
capital stock of K*, profits will be maximized since K* represents
a long-run equilibrium position for the economy. As the capital
stock increases beyond K_o, profits increase but at a diminishing
rate until the optimal capital stock is reached. The general
shape of the profitability curve is identical to that derived by
Eisner and Strotz.[2]

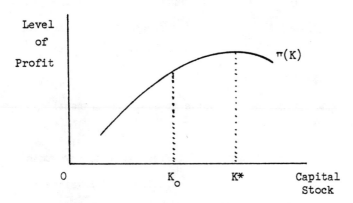

Fig. 11.--Profits as a function of the capital stock.

The Costs of Investment

If there were no cost to capital adjustment other than the

_____

[2]They assume that "the rate of profit earned by the firm may
...be regarded as a function of the size of the plant, since we may
assume that the amounts of the perfectly variable factors used with
a plant of given size are always optimally adjusted." R. Eisner and
R. Strotz, "Determinants of Business Investment," Commission on Money and Credit, Impacts of Monetary Policy (Englewood Cliffs, N.J:
Prentice-Hall, 1963), reprinted in A. Zellner, (ed.), Readings in
Economic Statistics and Econometrics (Boston: Little, Brown and
Company, 1968), pp. 463-515. p. 471.

normal operating cost, R, the story would end here. With a change
in output conditions indicating a higher rate of output, the
capital stock would immediately be adjusted to the new desired
level. However, as Eisner and Strotz point out, the adjustment
of the capital stock is seldom as rapid as possible. "The relative
fixity of various factors of production will cause the adjustment
to the ultimate, new equilibrium position to take place more or
less slowly."[3] The ultimate reason for a slower rather than a
more rapid accumulation of capital, however, is found in the
fact that it costs more to adjust the capital stock rapidly. In
fact, the reason capital is regarded as a fixed factor is not that
it can not be changed quickly, but that the cost of abandoning a
given stock of capital in favor of newer capital or of rapidly
acquiring more capital is too excessive to make the transition
economical.

Current literature on investment often explains investment
expenditures by employing the marginal efficiency of investment
(MEI) concept in conjunction with the marginal efficiency of
capital (MEC).[4] Both are related to the interest rate. The

---

[3]Ibid., p. 470.

[4]Keynes' original formulation used the term "marginal
efficiency of capital;" however, Keynes was speaking of investment expenditures. Keynes, The General Theory of Employment,
Interest and Money (New York: Harcourt, Brace & World, Inc.,
1964), pp. 135-136. Brooman and Jacoby, Macroeconomics: An
Introduction to Theory and Policy (Chicago: Aldine Publishing
Co., 1970) draw a distinction between MEC and MEI similar to
that given in the text. pp. 158-62. A.P. Lerner has a formulation
that uses both the MEC and the MEI in yet a different sense: "On
Some Recent Developments in Capital Theory," American Economic Review, LV (May, 1965), pp. 284-286.

intersection of the current interest rate and the MEC schedule
indicates the desired stock of capital. The intersection of the
MEI and the interest rate determines the actual rate of investment
which will take place in an attempt to obtain the desired stock
of capital. The concept of optimal stock of capital is similar
to the desired capital stock as determined by the intersection
of the MEC schedule and the interest rate. The MEC curve, however,
is drawn on the assumption that the rate of output is constant
while the interest rate varies. The marginal efficiency of
investment specifies the actual rate of investment as a function
of the interest rate for constant output levels. The investment
function assumes a given interest rate and specifies investment
levels under varying rates of final output.

In calculating the cost of investment an important factor
is, of course, the price of the investment goods. Both the interest
rate and the price of the capital good are used in determining
the current operating cost of capital. However, in the construction of the short-run average cost curve and the long-run average
cost curve, the current operating cost of capital, that is, the
interest rate and the price of the capital good, have been assumed
constant. The current operating cost used in these calculations
will be termed the "normal" cost of capital expansion. If there
were no additional costs encountered due to the rapidity of investment, this would be the only cost that need be considered. However, it will be assumed that any investment beyond that rate
necessary to maintain the existing capital stock, i.e. any net

investment, will encounter a capital cost function which increases with the desired increase in net capital.[5] There are a
number of reasons why the capital cost function would be expected
to increase with increasing net investment. The greater the
desired investment in any given period, the greater will be the
pressure on given resources and, hence, the greater the price
which must be paid to obtain new capital. This fact is reflected
in the higher aggregate price level which accompanies an expansion
in output beyond optimal capacity operation. The increase in
the price of the capital good will increase the current operating
costs and will be part of the premium capital cost function.

Monetary policy will also play a role in determining the
actual costs of capital expansion. If the monetary authorities
do not expand the money supply, then the increased demand for
investment goods in the face of a given supply of funds will lead
to an increase in the rate of interest. This increase in interest
rates can be viewed as part of the premium cost of capital expansion. In fact, the extreme assumption of a fixed money supply
can be relaxed and the same conclusions will be reached if only
the increasing demand for funds exceeds the supply. Another
cost which may be important and has been suggested by Eisner and
Strotz is the increased internal costs associated with the inte-

---

[5]This assumption is employed here since the present analysis
is static. In the context of growth, it might be assumed that any
investment over and above the normal investment for replacement and
"normal" growth in the economy would be subject to a premium cost
function, see below, Chap. V.

gration of new equipment. This would imply that a certain period of time is required before the flow variable, labor, can adopt itself to the new capital equipment and operate it at the level of efficiency for which it has been designed.[6] On all three counts above, the premium cost of net capital expansion rises as the desired rate of investment increases. In fact, it might also be expected that the rate of increase of the capital cost function would increase with larger and larger rates of desired investment. Fig. 12 illustrates the typical shape of the capital expansion cost function, $C(I)$.

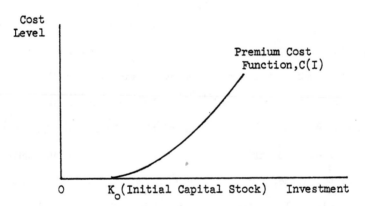

Fig. 12.--The probable shape of the premium cost function for rates of investment leading to net capital expansion.

Earlier analysis has indicated the relationship between potential profits and the desired stock of capital resulting from some change in the parameters of the system. These profit calculations include only the "normal" operating cost of capital. A

---

[6] Eisner and Strotz, op. cit., p. 479.

cost premium, over and above the normal operating cost will be incurred as the rate of expansion desired increases. This cost function will depend on the rate of change of capital, or the rate of investment, and the date at which delivery is expected.[7] The objective of the individual firm is the maximization of profits. Given a time horizon, it is reasonable to assume that firms attempt to maximize the net profitability of capital acquisition over time. This is equivalent to maximizing the functional ϕ, equation (4.1), where e^{-rt} is a discounting factor.

$$(4.1) \qquad \phi = \int_0^\infty e^{-rt} \left[\pi K(t) - C(K,t) \right] dt$$

Although it is a drastic jump to go from the assumption of individual firm profit maximization to the assumption that the aggregate economy proceeds in the same manner, nevertheless, the transition is not unprecedented[8] and this assumption will be adopted here. For the economy then, the solution of the functional ϕ yields a path of capital expansion over time from one equilibrium position to another. This problem in the calculus of variations has been admirably solved by Eisner and Strotz.[9] Fig. 13

---

[7]It might be expected that orders placed now would have lower costs associated with them if delivery were not required in the present time period.

[8]"It is admittedly a bold stroke for us to regard the individual firm of our model as a minature of an entire industry or of the economy. But this we do." Eisner and Strotz, op. cit., p. 480.

[9]Ibid., Appendix A, pp. 510-512.

illustrates a typical solution indicating the actual stock of
capital as a function of time, t, as the capital stock changes
from an initial level K_o to a new "desired" level, K^*.[10]

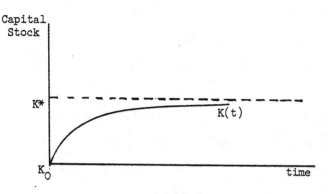

Fig. 13.--The expansion path of the capital stock
as it adjusts to a new equilibrium level.

The Derivation of an Investment Function

Interest in this study does not center on the adjustment
through time of the capital stock, but rather on the investment
rate applicable during the current period. In Fig. 14, the
profit and cost functions of capital expansion are combined.
In the case illustrated, it is clear that it would not pay to
expand the capital stock immediately to the new optimum level
since the cost premium would be so high that most of the potential
profitability would be eliminated. The net profitability of capital
expansion in the first period, the difference between the profit
and cost functions, is maximized somewhere short of K^*. Just

---

[10]Fig. 13 is adopted from Ibid., Fig. 2, p. 478.

precisely where is obtained by the solution of equation (4.1).
Intuitively, the solution will require that the marginal increase
in the profitability of capital expansion should just equal the
marginal increase in the cost of acquiring that capital. In
other words, the level of investment is determined by the maximum
distance between the profit and cost functions of Fig. 14. This
maximum distance is found where the slope of the profit function,
the marginal profitability of investment, is just equal to the
slope of the premium cost function, the marginal cost of investment. Investment in the first period under the conditions
assumed in Fig. 14 would be represented by I_1.

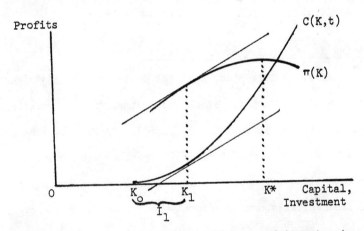

Fig. 14.--The determination of the optimal rate of investment.

The desired rate of investment relative to one particular
rate of output, i.e. that rate which makes K* the optimal capital
stock, has been determined. It remains to specify the desired
rate of investment for all possible rates of output both above and
below the current "optimal" rate. When this has been accomplished,

an aggregate investment function relating rates of investment to rates of output will have been derived.

  With any particular rate of output, a definite optimal capital stock will be indicated and to each optimal capital stock will correspond a definite profitability function. Thus a whole family of profitability functions exist, each one defined by the difference between the current stock and the optimal capital stock. In Fig. 15 a series of different aggregate expenditure curves has been drawn to represent different rates of expenditure in the face of a given supply function. The initial position of the variables is represented by the subscript "o". Assume a shift in aggregate expenditure from D_o to D_1. Output rises in the short-run to X_1 and the optimal capital stock becomes K_1. For this new optimal capital stock a specific profitability function exists and is represented by $\pi(K_1)$ in the third quadrant. (To concentrate entirely on the potential profitability of investment, the profitability functions all start from zero. They thus indicate the addition to total profits due to an increase in the capital stock.)

  The profit function appropriate to the rate of expenditure D_1 is, of course, maximized at a capital stock of K_1. A similar analysis can be made for other rates of aggregate expenditure, D_2 to D_4. Each rate of aggregate expenditure results in a current rate of output which determines a new desired stock of capital. To each desired stock of capital corresponds a specific profitability function. The further output moves above its current optimal rate;

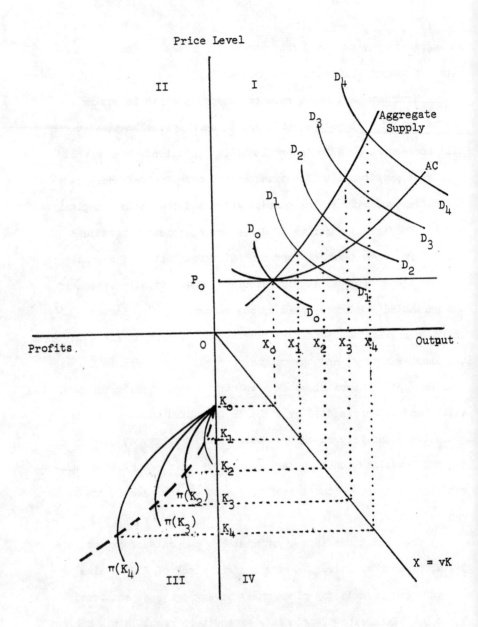

Fig. 15.--Changes in Aggregate Expenditure and the resulting changes in the profitability of investment.

that is, the greater the distance between actual output, X, and the rate of output appropriate to the existing stock of capital, X_o, the greater will be the potential profitability of adjusting the capital stock. This is signified in the third quadrant where the dotted line represents the locus of all the maximum points of the family of profit potential curves.

It is clear from the diagram that the profit curve is related to the distance between the current stock of capital and the desired stock of capital. This fact can be used to illustrate the rates of investment as an economy approaches its desired capital stock. In Fig. 16, a change in the rate of final output has increased the desired capital stock from K_o to K^*. The premium cost of investment can be represented by $C(\dot{K}) = C(I)$; assume also that this function is independent of the difference between actual and desired capital stocks. By the analysis of the previous section, the optimal rate of investment in the first period is given by I_1 and the capital stock increases to K_1. With the new capital stock, the optimal rate of output has increased and hence the difference between the current rate and the current optimal rate has narrowed. Thus, the profitability function shifts downward to the position indicated by $\pi(K_1)$. Investment in the second period is given by I_2 with the capital stock advancing to K_2. The process continues and, as the actual stock of capital nears the desired stock, the profits to be gained by extra investment gradually diminish and hence, the rate of net investment itself diminishes until the

desired stock of capital is attained. Note that this type of
behavior over time is precisely that implied by the capital stock
path derived by Eisner and Strotz and illustrated in Fig. 13, p. 77.

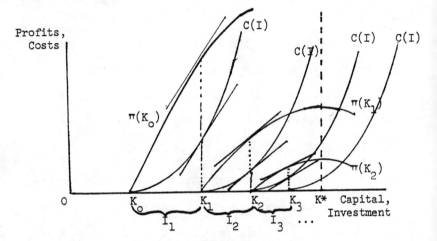

Fig. 16.--Gradual adjustment of the capital stock to its
desired level, K*.

Fig. 16 describes the investment rates over time as the
capital stock adjusts to a new equilibrium level. A slight
modification, however, will be sufficient to obtain the investment function at any moment of time. In Fig. 17, a whole family
of profit curves is drawn originating at the current capital stock
K_o. Each profit curve corresponds to a specific desired capital
stock and hence a specific rate of current output. The higher are
the profit curves, the greater is the actual rate of output above
the optimal rate for the given stock of capital. The costs of
capital expansion are represented by C(I) and it is assumed that
these costs are independent of the level of actual capacity
operation. For each of the different levels of capacity operation,

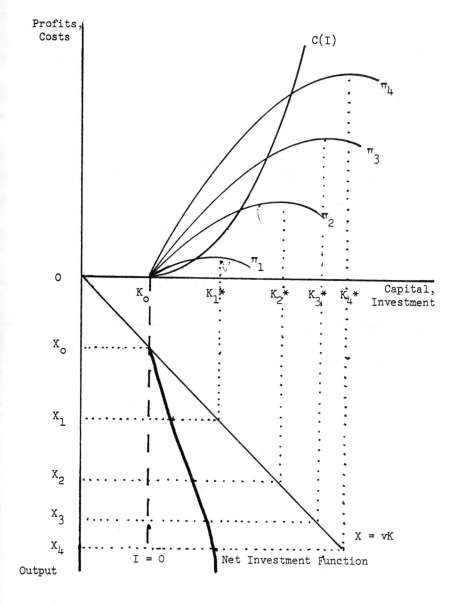

Fig. 17.--The derivation of the net investment function.

a specific rate of investment can be determined. The desired
rate of investment increases as the actual rate of output exceeds
the current optimal rate. However, due to the capital cost function
there is a limit to the amount of investment desired in any given
period. No matter how far output expands beyond the optimal capacity,
a point will be reached where the increasing acquisition cost of
new capital equipment will limit the first period's investment.
This is not necessarily a physical limitation to the production
of capital goods, but rather an economic one. Note that in Fig. 17
the amount of investment increases with the increase in desired
capital, but is eventually choked off due to the increasing cost
function. The slope of the investment function is positive, and
the second derivative negative. How far output must be above the
optimal rate of capacity before increases in investment become
negligible will depend on the particular nature of the cost
function assumed. In fact, if there were no premium costs to
capital expansion, the investment function would increase con-
tinuously with the rate of output.

In the analysis to follow, concentration will be centered
on gross rather than net investment. There are two primary
reasons for this decision. First, it is questionable whether in
practice it is possible to distinguish between net and replacement
investment. Secondly, it often happens that firms install larger
or better machines when replacing worn-out capital. "Replacement
is seldom made without improvement. A worn-out piece of equipment is rarely replaced with an identical item."[11] Thus, when

examining either the demand-generating or capacity-generating effects of investment, it is gross investment which should be considered. In Fig. 18 the net investment function is converted to a gross investment function. With a current stock of capital K_o, the optimal rate of output is X_o. Investment at an output rate of X_o will be I_o which is just sufficient to maintain the existing stock of capital, or, if new capital is more efficient, just sufficient to maintain the output capacity of the existing stock of capital. I_o represents total gross investment; net investment is, of course, zero. As the actual rate of output expands beyond the optimal, the rate of investment increases until it reaches the maximum one period rate of investment, I'.

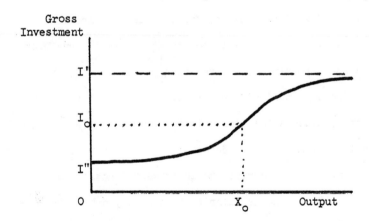

Fig. 18.--Gross investment function, preliminary form.

Little attention has been directed to output rates below

[11]W.W.Heller, "The Anatomy of Investment Decisions," Harvard Business Review, (March, 1951), p. 100.

the optimal. When aggregate demand decreases causing a reduction
in the aggregate price level and the rate of output, firms within
the economy will be sustaining losses. The actual return to
capital will be below the current operating cost. The capital
stock will be excessive and producers will attempt to adjust
the capital stock to the new desired level. However, downward
adjustments are limited by an absolute floor on gross investment
of zero. Disinvestment is thus limited by the rate of depreciation.
In fact, it is reasonable to assume that some part of gross investment expenditure is independent of actual capacity operation.
This "autonomous' investment, therefore, provides a floor for
the gross investment function represented by I" in Fig. 18.

The derived gross investment function is non-linear and
bears a striking graphical resemblance to others which have been
developed in the literature. Before going on to refine further
the aggregate investment function, therefore, it would be useful
at this point to discuss the similarities, and the differences,
between the investment function developed here and earlier functions.

The method used to derive the investment function in this
paper is outwardly somewhat similar to that employed by Dale Jorgenson in his "Anticipations and Investment Behavior."[12] He
assumes that firms attempt to maximize net worth over time.

─────────────

[12]Dale W. Jorgenson, "Anticipations and Investment
Behavior," in The Brookings Quarterly Econometric Model of
the United States, J. Duesenberry, G. Fromm, L. Klein, and
E. Kuh (eds.) (Chicago: Rand McNally & Company, 1965),
pp. 35-94.

His marginal productivity conditions imply, as do those here, that
the marginal revenue product of capital should be equal to the
current operating cost (Jorgenson uses the term "user cost") of
capital. The actual rate of investment is a function of actual
and desired capital stocks, although the manner in which current
investment depends on these variables is radically different in
the two studies because of major differences in basic assumptions.
In his net worth formula, Jorgenson takes explicit consideration
of the impact of varying tax rates, but he does not consider any
possible alteration in the cost of investment goods subsequent
to changes in the rate of investment. Jorgenson specifies a
separate theory of investment for capital expansion and for
replacement investment. He assumes, without strong justification,
that all past capital investments will automatically be replaced
when they wear out. Investment for expansion, on the other hand,
is given by a distributed lag function of the difference between
any two periods in desired capital stock levels. That conclusion
rests on the assumption that the actual capital stock at the end
of any period plus the backlog of investment projects yet to be
completed is equal to the desired capital stock at the beginning
of the period. It certainly is not clear that actual capital
stocks plus backlogs of investment can reach the desired level of
capital stock within a single period. Nor is it reasonable to
assume that the investment resulting from a difference of z units
in desired capital stocks will be the same regardless of the
current capacity position of the firm.

The Kaldor Investment Function

Nicholas Kaldor specifies a non-linear investment function which, on the surface, seems identical to that developed in this paper. However, there are several important differences. Kaldor defines his investment function in terms of the level of activity where by "activity" is meant the level of employment. His function specifies the change in investment as a function of the change in activity:

> ...In the case of the investment function it is probable that dI/dx will be <u>small</u>, both for low and for high levels of x [in Kaldor's notation, x, represents the level of activity which would correspond with the L used to indicate labor input in the present analysis] , relatively to its "normal" level. It will be small for low levels of activity because when there is a great deal of surplus capacity, an increase in activity will not induce entrepreneurs to under-take additional construction: the rise in profits will not stimulate investment. (At the same time, the level of investment will not be zero, for there is always some in-vestment undertaken for long-period development purposes which is independent of current activity.) But it will also be small for unusually high levels of activity, because rising costs of construction, increasing costs and increasing difficulty of borrowing will dissuade entrepreneurs from expanding still faster--at a time when they already have large committments.[13]

The investment function of Fig. 18, p. 85, defined in terms of the rate of real output rather than the level of employ-ment, displays the same slope characteristics of the Kaldor func-tion for "high" and "low" rates of real output, and for basically the same reasons as those Kaldor offers for his function. Indeed,

---

[13]N. Kaldor, "A Model of the Trade Cycle," <u>Economic Journal</u>, XLIX (March, 1940), p. 81.

the Kaldor function can be derived from the present investment
function as illustrated in Fig. 19. The initial capital stock
is K_o and with factor prices given by the line mm in the third
quadrant, the optimal rate of output would be X_o. Thus, the
aggregate investment function developed above is defined and is
drawn in the first quadrant. At point A, gross investment is
just sufficient to maintain the capital stock at K_o. The amount
of labor employed at an output rate of X_o is given by L_o. The
combination of L_o and I_o determine one point on Kaldor's function:
point A' in the second quadrant. To obtain other points, consider
a rate of output given by X_1. Investment is given by point B.
To find the corresponding point on the Kaldor function, it
must be determined what amount of labor would be employed at an
output rate of X_1. In the fourth quadrant the line $K = vX$ determines the relationship between capital and output if the economy
is on its expansion path, OE, in the third quadrant. Thus at an
output rate of X_1, the desired capital stock would be K_1. The
isoquant which intersects the expansion path, OE, in the third
quadrant at a capital stock of K_1 determines, therefore, the rate
of output X_1 in the isoquant map.

There are now two possibilities for the labor input. If
the capital stock is fully employed, the economy will be operating
at point B'" and the labor input will be L_1. On the other hand,
if the economy operates with fixed coefficients in production
for output levels which do not use the capital stock entirely,
the labor input might be represented by L_1'. In either case the

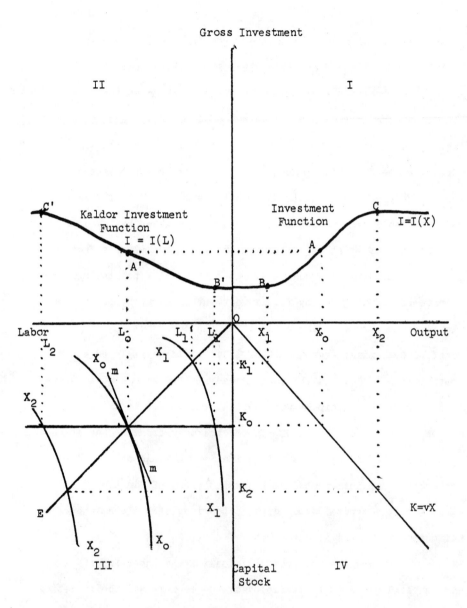

Fig. 19.--The derivation of the Kaldor Investment Function
from the gross investment function developed here.

shape of the Kaldor function would be little affected. In this paper, it has been assumed that the significance of capital is found predominantly in its presence in production, i.e. that the economy is operating at point B'". Other points on the Kaldor function are found in a similar manner. For the rate of output X_2, the desired capital stock is K_2 which, in conjunction with the expansion path in quadrant III, determines the X_2 isoquant. The actual stock of capital and the X_2 isoquant meet at point C". The labor input is L_2 and the point on the Kaldor function is C'. The Kaldor function corresponding to the aggregate investment function developed in this chapter is thus derived in the second quadrant.

The difficulty in the Kaldorian function is that it is tied to such concepts as "normal" level of activity and relatively high and low levels of activity. Precisely what determines normality is never defined. If activity is interpreted as the level of employment, what is a "normal" level? In the derivation here, the "normal" level of activity is that level of employment which, given the factor prices in the economy--parameters which Kaldor ignores--and given the stock of capital, produces a flow of output at the minimum average cost level. It is not at all clear that this is what Kaldor meant to imply by normal level of activity. To imply that the normal level of employment is in terms of absolute numbers overlooks the fact that the labor force is not stationary, but rather grows over time. With a growing population, no absolute level of employment can be regarded as normal.

If instead of absolute levels, the normal level of
activity is defined as some percentage of employment, further
difficulties arise. In the derivation in Fig. 19, the full-
employment level of the labor force had not been specified.
Full-employment could be represented by L_o or by any level of
labor employment beyond L_o. In the present model, the optimal
labor input given the capital stock can represent anywhere from
full-employment of the labor force to large-scale unemployment.
These considerations lead to a rejection of the attempt to define
an aggregate investment function in terms of the level of
employment.

The Vanek Investment Function

Jaroslav Vanek has derived an aggregate investment function,
based on very different assumptions, that is almost identical to
that derived here. Vanek feels that in the short-run with the
capital stock fixed, a production function with approximately
fixed coefficients is the relevant one. Thus, in Fig. 20 (a),
with the capital stock at K_o and full-employment of labor at L_o,
factor inputs for rates of output below X_o, i.e. at less than
full-employment, are found along the line OA rather than, as in
the model developed here, the line K_oA. The result is that for
output rates below X_o both part of the labor force and part of
the capital stock are unemployed. The existence of unemployed
capital results in a very low marginal efficiency of investment.
When output, however, is near X_o where all of the capital stock
is utilized, the marginal efficiency of investment becomes quite

high. The aggregate investment function is then derived from
this difference in the marginal efficiency of investment between
low levels of capacity utilization and full capacity operation.
The investment function, however, does not display a marked discontinuity since entrepreneurs "base their decisions also on
longer range expectations, the availability of funds, the rate of
interest, etc. A rational entrepreneur operating in time will not
wait to place new orders until his last piece of equipment is
fully employed."[14] The result of these qualifications will be
simply to round off the edges of the discontinuity in the investment function. Fig. 20 (b) illustrates Vanek's investment
function.

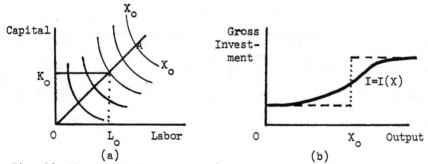

(a)   (b)

Fig. 20--The derivation of Vanek's Investment function.

Vanek's investment function, although it is defined for
real rates of output, is based on the degree of capacity utilization. With large levels of unused capacity, investment is quite
low. Investment here must be considered gross investment since

[14] J. Vanek, "The Labor Market, Technology, and Stability in
the Keynesian Model," Kyklos, XVI (1963), p. 115.

net investment would be expected to be negative in the presence of large amounts of excess capacity. With the capital stock fully utilized, output at X_o, Vanek assumes that the marginal efficiency of investment is high. However, the fact that capital is being fully employed in the extreme fixed-coefficient case is not a sufficient justification to assume that a larger stock of capital is required. If X_o is the rate of real output demanded at going prices, any increase in the capital stock would only lead to the creation of excess capacity. In determining investment expenditure, both the degree of excess capacity and the expected demand for real output must be taken into consideration.

Vanek's function would be more realistic if it assumed, even though production might be subject to fixed coefficients, a certain degree of desired excess capacity. Chenery has shown that, in fact, this is the case in industries which display increasing returns to scale, and Smith has extended this result to the case of constant returns to scale.[15] Thus, it might be assumed that, for example, 90 per cent of capacity was the optimal degree of capital utilization. When output was at a rate sufficient to attain 90 per cent of capacity utilization, investment would be equal to depreciation of the capital stock. For output rates above 90 per cent, however, gross investment

---

[15]H. Chenery, "Overcapacity and the Acceleration Principle," Econometrica, XX (Jaunary, 1950), pp. 1-28; V. Smith, Investment and Production (Cambridge: Harvard University Press, 1966), pp. 286-89.

would exceed replacement and there would be a growth in the capital stock. Using this assumption, there would be a rationale for expecting gross investment to be quite high when the capital stock became fully employed.

A critical point of Vanek's article is that with the above non-linear investment function, an unstable equilibrium will be found in the vicinity of full capacity use of capital. This results from the fact that the slope of the investment function exceeds the slope of the savings function, Fig. 21. There are three possible equilibriums represented by the points A, B, and C. Points A and C are stable while B is an unstable equilibrium. If full-capacity output is represented by FC, the stable equilibrium point C is unattainable since, under the assumption of fixed coefficients, no further output is attainable. If it is assumed that 90 per cent represents the optimal capacity operation, point B, it would appear that, even though the economy were operating at the desired rate of output, the equilibrium would be unstable. Output would either have to expand to the full capacity level where it would encounter a ceiling due to the shortage of capital stock, or fall back to the stable equilibrium point A, a situation of large excess capacity. This instability in the face of a situation where the desired stock of capital is equal to the current stock is a disturbing element in the analysis. Before discussing it further, however, the derivation of the aggregate investment function employed in this model must be completed.

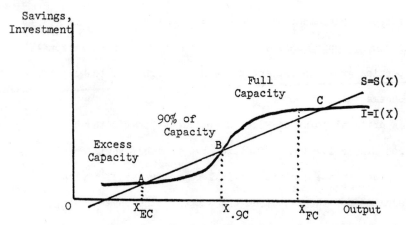

Fig. 21.--Possible short-run equilibrium positions in the Vanek investment function.

Financing Investment Expenditures

The above derivation of the aggregate investment function illustrated in Fig. 18, p. 85, has been based on a very simple assumption concerning the premium costs inherent in rapid capital expansion. In order to bring the analysis somewhat closer to reality, however, the shape of the premium cost function must be carefully considered. To examine this cost function more closely will require a review of the sources and costs of investment financing facing the individual firm.[16]

A simplified analysis of investment expenditure assumes that the amount of investment expenditures is given by the inter-section of the MEI schedule and the rate of interest. With a

---

[16] This discussion owes much to J. Duesenberry, Business Cycles and Economic Growth (New York: McGraw-Hill Book Co., 1958); see especially Chap. 5, "Sources of Funds and the Cost of Capital," pp. 87-112.

constant rate of interest, therefore, the determinants of investment expenditure would be basically the factors which cause a
shift in the MEI schedule, a major factor, of course, being the
current or expected rate of output. There would be little to
prevent firms from exploiting all investment opportunities encountered. The actual movement of investment expenditures,
however, seems to be one of a lag behind the years in which investment opportunities are large to years when activity has slowed.
Duesenberry sees the explanation of this phenomenon in the
limitations in the supply of money capital.[17] In fact, a number
of studies have arisen which support the importance of financial
factors in determining the rate of investment.[18] These lead to a
conclusion that the supply of funds or capital to the firm is not
perfectly elastic. Rather it displays discontinuities, or perhaps
rapid changes, as firms switch from one particular form of financing
to another.

Assume that the supply of investment funds is composed of

---

[17]Ibid., p. 88-89.

[18]See, for example, J. Meyer and E. Kuh, "Acceleration and
Related Theories of Investment," Review of Economics and Statistics,
XXXVII (August, 1955), pp. 217-230; J. Meyer and E. Kuh, The Invest-
ment Decision (Cambridge: Harvard University Press, 1957). Another
cross-section study of investment behavior which found profits im-
portant in investment is L.R.Klein, "Studies in Investment Behavior,"
Conference on Business Cycles (New York: National Bureau of Economic
Research, 1951). For time series analysis see L.R. Klein and A.S.
Goldberger, An Econometric Model of the United States 1929-1952
(Amsterdam: North-Holland Publishing Co., 1955) and J. Tinbergen,
Business Cycles in the United States 1919-1932 (Geneva: League
of Nations, 1939).

three elements: (1) retained earnings and depreciation allowances, (2) borrowing, and (3) issuance of new equities. The
exact costs of finance will depend on the particular source of
investment financing employed, and the attitudes of management
toward the assumption of risk. In the extreme case, assume that
management has a strong aversion to any debt financing. The
supply of funds schedule of such a firm appears in Fig. 22 (a).[19]
The amount of retained earnings and depreciation allowances is
given by OA. The cost of using internal funds to finance investment is the foregone opportunity cost of investing the funds in
securities outside the firm. Assume that this opportunity cost
is equal to the interest rate the firm would have to pay if it
issued its own debt, adjusted for the fact that interest earnings
are subject to the corporate income tax. If the interest rate
is 6% and the corporate income tax is 50%, then the opportunity
cost of internal funds is 3%. Once internal funds have been
exhausted, new finance would be available only by issuing new
equities which, at the going market price, might cost 6%. The
supply of funds schedule, assuming the firm does no borrowing,
is the broken line segment BCDE. When the firm is shifting from
internal finance to equity financing, there is a discontinuity.
The result is that there must be a considerable shift in the MEI
schedule to have any effect on actual investment expenditures.

---

[19] Fig. 22 (a) and (c) and the discussion on internal
financing is adopted from W. Smith, Macroeconomics (Homewood, Ill.:
Richard D. Irwin, 1970), Ch. 10, Fig. 10-1, p. 198.

Assuming that an increase in the rate of output shifts the
MEI to the right, the investment expenditure of the firm relative
to the rate of output is given in Fig. 22 (b). As the rate of
output increases to x_2, investment expenditures increase steadily.
However, increases in output from x_2 to x_3 have no effect on
investment expenditures which remain at the limit of internal
financing, OA. With output increases beyond x_3, the investment
schedule once more increases with output.

In Fig. 22 (c) the assumption of a strong aversion to
borrowing is dropped. Thus, the firm is willing to borrow funds
for investment financing and, in fact, most firms will be inclined
to borrow before attempting additional finance through equity
issue.[20] The segment BC represents the funds available through
internal financing while the curved segment CD represents borrowing.
In addition to the interest which must be paid, it is assumed that
firms impute additional costs attributable to the risks associated

---

[20]Smith lists a number of reasons for primary reliance on
debt financing: "First, interest on loans or bonds is a deductible
expense in calculating income under the corporate income tax,
whereas dividends paid on stock are not deductible. With combined federal and state corporate income tax rates of around 50
percent, the deductibility of interest sharply biases financing
decisions toward issuance of debt rather than equities. In addition,
the financial institutions, notably life insurance companies, that
have traditionally been the main suppliers of long-term funds to
corporations are much more disposed to invest in bonds, which pay
a fixed income, than in stocks. And finally, sale of new voting
stock to outsiders may weaken the position of the group currently
controlling the corporation. It is important to note that reten-
tion of earnings adds to the equity capital of the corporation,
but, unlike the sale of new stock to outsiders, leaves the control
of the corporation undisturbed." Ibid., p. 196.

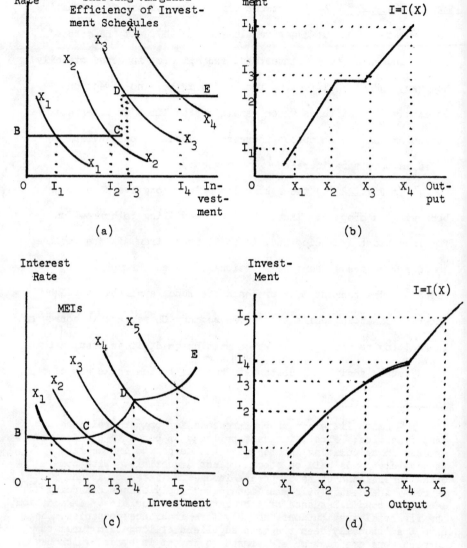

Fig. 22.--The relationship between the supply of funds schedule and the investment function.

with borrowing. These additional costs rise as the amount of
debt increases, since firms will calculate higher risk premiums
on increasing debt-equity ratios. When the explicit interest
cost together with the imputed costs rises to 6% (point D), it
now becomes worthwhile to finance by selling new stock. The
segment DE slopes upward in Fig. 22 (c) since allowance is made
for the fact that sale of additional stock is likely to cause a
decline in the price of stock and hence will entail increasing
costs with the amount of stock put on sale.

The supply of funds schedule of Fig. 22 (c) is translated
into the investment-output plane in Fig. 22 (d). Investment will
increase steadily with the increase in output up to x_2. Increases
in output from x_2 to x_4 do not stop investment entirely; however,
the proportional increase slows down as the cost of borrowing
rises. For output rates beyond x_4 investment expenditures will
once more increase with output until the cost of equity financing
increases to prohibitive rates (the slope of the segment DE in
Fig. 22 (c) increases to plus infinity) at which point increases
in investment expenditures are choked off.

The Adjusted Cost of Expansion Function

The effect of these considerations on the aggregate premium
cost function is illustrated in Fig. 23. Originally with a capital
stock of K_o, the premium cost function was assumed to increase at
an increasing rate for any net investment beyond K_o. To consider gross investment, assume that the capital stock during a
given period depreciates to the level K_o'. Thus the gross invest-

ment necessary to increase the capital stock back to K_o is
represented by the segment $(K_o - K_o')$. Premium costs of this
gross investment are assumed to be zero, that is, gross investment
which replaces the capital stock is obtainable at the "standard"
interest cost used in the calculation of R in current operating
cost. In terms of the individual firm analysis, this gross
investment which is financed out of depreciation allowances
entails the smallest cost in the supply of funds schedule.
Investment, however, which requires financing from external sources
involves an increase in cost, in fact, a discontinuous increase
in cost. This is represented by the shift of the premium cost
function upward from $C(K)$ to $C'(K)$. From the factors discussed
earlier, it is clear that this upward increase in costs need not
be a sharp break, but is more likely a continuous, although rapid,
increase in costs represented by the curved section of $C'(\dot{K})$ in
Fig. 23.

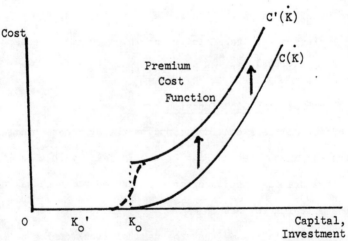

Fig. 23.--The discontinuity of the Premium cost function.

The sharp increase in costs as the economy shifts from capital replacement to net capital expansion is due not only to the increased financing costs, but also in part to other factors. There is likely to be an increase in internal costs. The acquisition of new capital entails the disruption of the normal productive process: workers must be hired and trained, managers must learn to cope with the new techniques, develop new outlets for the product, etc.[21] Another factor to consider is that capital equipment may be bulky and the employment of additional capital justified only when output has increased considerably.[22] It should be noted at this stage that this increase in cost as the firms shift from capital replacement to capital expansion is tied to the static analysis of the present chapter. In the following chapter, when dynamic implications are explored, it will be seen that the lower costs of capital replacement are reasonably extended into a "normal" degree of capital expansion which might be related to the observed long-run

---

[21]T. Hultgren, American Transportation in Prosperity and Depression (New York, 1948) has stated that because of this management cost "no one railroad typically buys cars in continuous driblets; or at any rate small repetitive purchases can hardly account for any large part of total orders." p. 167. See also W.W.Heller, op. cit.,p. 102: "One of the unforeseen--and most interesting--investment barriers was the bottleneck in top engineering and management talent."

[22]"For example, paper-making machines for the manufacture of newsprint paper come only in million dollar units capable of producing one-fourth the requirements of a good-sized plant and characterized by great durability." C.D.Long, Building Cycles and the Theory of Investment (Princeton: Princeton University Press, 1940), pp. 61-2.

growth experienced by the economy. The premium costs there will
then be associated with increases in the capital stock which
exceed the normal expected increase.

Aggregate Investment Function: Final Form

What effect, if any, would this discontinuity, or break,
in the premium cost function have on the aggregate investment
function? In Fig. 24, a family of profitability curves has been
drawn with the new premium cost function (PCF). The derived
investment function is found in the bottom half of the figure.
Assume that the current stock of capital can be represented by
K_0. The current and potential profitability of production depends
on the current rate of output. If the current rate of output is
the optimal rate, X_0 in Fig. 24, then there will be no "economic"
profits being earned in the community; both capital and labor will
be receiving their marginal products. Suppose now that output
increases to x_4. The desired capital stock becomes K_4^*. The
profitability of investment is indicated by the π_4 curve. Positive
profits are now being earned with the current capital stock, but
these could be increased if the current stock were K_4^*, assuming
no other costs. However, there are other costs represented by
the PCF. The increase in capital cost due to net expansion
eradicates the profitability of expanding the capital stock to
K_4^*. The net profitability of expansion, the distance between
π_4 and $C'(K)$, is never greater than the profit already being earned
with the current capital stock, K_0. For the investment function,
then, net investment at an output rate X_4 is the same as at X_0, zero.

If the capital stock desired increases to K_5^* or K_6^*, however, the profitability of investment improves. If output has increased to X_5, the profitability of capital expansion exceeds the current level of profits. The actual rate of investment is determined by the maximum vertical distance between π_5 and $C'(K)$. Thus, for output rates above the optimal, the investment function, although it may be little affected by slight increases, will eventually indicate higher investment rates with higher levels of output. The presence of a PCF, on the other hand, assures that the increases in investment expenditures in the given period must level off to some maximum rate.

To examine the shape of the investment curve for decreases in output, consider the profit functions π_1 through π_3. If the actual rate of output falls below the optimal, say to X_3, the current stock of capital will exceed the optimal. There will be excess capacity and the capital will be receiving less than its marginal product. Economic losses will thus be encountered if the current stock of capital is maintained. These losses, however, can be minimized by decreasing the capital stock to its new desired level. If it is assumed that there is no additional cost encountered in the process of capital depreciation, net investment would be given by the negative distance from K_0 to K_3^*. In this situation, the economy can adjust in a single period to the new desired capital stock. Although there are no additional costs encountered under disinvestment, there is a limit to the amount of capital that can be eliminated in any one period. This limit

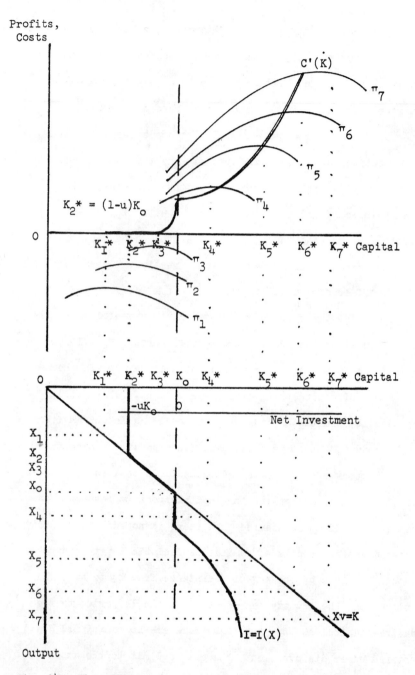

Fig. 24.--The effect of a discontinuity in the premium cost function on the aggregate investment function.

is given by the rate of depreciation. If the rate of depreciation
is represented by $\underline{u}$, then the maximum disinvestment in a single
period is given by uK_o. In Fig. 24, therefore, any desired
capital stock between K_2* (assumed equal to $K_o - uK_o$) and K_o
can be attained in a single period by disinvestment. In the
investment function, this is represented by the segment between
the rate of output X_2 and X_o. If the rate of output should fall
all the way to X_1, the desired capital stock falls to K_1*. But
the rate of disinvestment is limited to uK_o. Therefore, the
investment function levels off for all output rates below X_2.

The sharp discontinuity in the investment function of
Fig. 24 is, of course, an extreme case and highly unrealistic.
Thus, in depicting the revised aggregate investment function in
Fig. 25, the discontinuity has been modified into a rapid rise
in investment expenditure. Assume that the optimal rate of
output is X_o and that gross investment at that rate of output is
given by a rate of investment of I_1. If the actual rate of output is in the neighborhood of X_o, say anywhere between X_1 and X_2,
the effect on investment expenditures will be negligible. K_o will
remain the desired stock of capital. However, if actual output
is beyond X_2, then there will be a sharp increase in investment
expenditures which would continue to increase indefinitely with
increases in output but not for the economic limitation placed on
the rate of investment possible in any given period. This limit
to investment expenditures is represented by I_2. Similarly, for
decreases in output, minor changes in actual output moving it

below the optimal rate will not result in an immediate re-
evaluation of the desired capital stock. However, major reductions will call forth net disinvestment of the capital stock
which, for low levels of output would fall to its extreme value
of zero except for the autonomous component in investment expenditure represented by I_1.

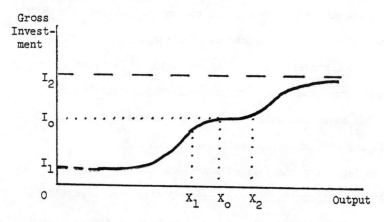

Fig. 25.--Aggregate Investment Function: Final Form.

In the static analysis, it has implicitly been assumed
that entrepreneurs anticipate the current rate of output to
maintain itself. This assumption must be modified to consider
growth possibilities since it is quite unrealistic in a dynamic
context. Expectations of future output will govern investment
decisions. It is reasonable to assume that entrepreneurs base
their decisions and what the desired stock of capital is in the
coming period on what they expect the rate of output to be in
that period. Their expectations of next period's output are
likely to be based on some weighted average of past rates of

output. If this is true, the argument for a low marginal propensity
to invest in the neighborhood of equilibrium output is reinforced.
If expected output is the relevant argument in investment decisions,
then a current rate of output very near the optimal rate, when
averaged over past rates of output at the optimal rate, will have
a negligible effect on net investment. By the same token, if
current output is significantly greater than past rates, even a
weighted average would indicate that expected output levels have
increased and investment will be adjusted accordingly. The same
conclusions hold, of course, for rates of output below the optimum.
If the rate of output is 99 and the optimal rate is 100, one would
not expect firms to revise drastically their expectations of next
period's output. However, if the actual rate of output is 80
when the optimal rate is 100, replacement decisions might very
well be affected.[23]

The specific range of output rates around the equilibrium
rate for which the marginal propensity to invest is low will
depend on a number of factors. One, of course, is the size of
the discontinuity in the premium capital acquisition costs. If
the difference between internal and external financing is insig-
nificant, then net capital expansion could be financed at the same

---

[23]"Regardless of the state of present demand, entrepreneurs
will not increase present capacity unless their anticipations
for the future warrant the step." A.S.Manne, "Some Notes on the
Acceleration Principle, Review of Economics and Statistics, XXVII
(1945), p. 89, fn.

rate as capital replacement. However, as the spread between internal and external financing increases, the degree to which current output must exceed optimal output before capital expansion will take place will also increase.

The past history of output fluctuations within the economy will also be important in determining the range of low investment propensities. If output has tended to fluctuate widely from one period to another, then firms will be quite reluctant to take any small increase in the rate of output as an indication that capital expansion is required. On the other hand, if the rate of final output, or more realistically, the rate of growth of the rate of final output, has been relatively stable, then only small changes in the actual rate of output above or below the expected rate will be needed to induce changes in the aggregate rate of investment.

Chapter V

COMPARATIVE STATICS AND DYNAMICS

Summary of the Basic Model

The main components of the short-run model implied by
the development of Chapters II through IV might usefully be
reviewed at this stage. Aggregate supply and aggregate expenditure jointly determine the actual rate of output and the price
level in the economy. Aggregate supply is assumed to be a function of the existing stock of capital, the prices of capital and
of labor, and the level of technology in the economy. Equation
(5.1) represents the aggregate supply curve where T is used to

$$(5.1) \qquad X_s = X_s(W,R,K,T)$$

technology parameters. If a Cobb-Douglas production function
is assumed, although this is not a requirement of the model,
the technology parameters could be represented more explicitly
by the elasticity of output with respect to capital and with
respect to labor, α and β, and shifts of the production function, A:

$$(5.2) \qquad X = A \, K^\alpha \, L^\beta$$

The aggregate supply curve relates real output supplied to the
price level. Prices, however, depend on the costs of production
and, since these are represented by the variables included in (5.1),
it is unnecessary to include a specific term for prices.

The rate of aggregate expenditure depends on the real

111

demand in the economy, X_d, and the expected level of prices, P_e

Equation (5.3) specifies the definition of aggregate expenditure.

$$(5.3) \qquad D = P_e X_d = M_d \overline{V}$$

The term for the expected level of prices, P_e, is employed to
convert the components of real demand into corresponding monetary
aggregates. Any one of a number of assumptions about the expected
price level is possible. It might be assumed that the current
price level is expected to continue or perhaps that the current
rate of change in prices, if any, is expected to continue.
Actual expectations will probably be a complicated function of
past prices and price movements. The exact specification is not
critical for present purposes.

Aggregate expenditure is also, by definition, equal to the
current money stock, M_d, times the velocity of circulation, V.
For simplicity, the velocity of money has been assumed constant,
hence $\overline{V}$ in equation (5.3). M_d represents the stock of money
necessary to transform the real elements in demand into a form
in which they can be realized. To avoid the complications of
monetary policy at this stage, it is assumed that the supply of
money, M_s, provided by the banking system is always equivalent to
what consumers and investors believe is necessary, equation (5.4).

$$(5.4) \qquad M_s = M_d$$

All funds desired at existing interest rates are supplied by
the monetary authorities.

Since government has been ignored in the model, the com-

ponents of real demand are given by the sum of real consumption
and real investment demand. Consumption demand is assumed to
be a function of the rate of real income, X, and the net worth
of consumers in the economy. Although the net worth component
can be complicated by intricate financial portfolio analysis,
in the present context it is simply assumed that the only form
in which wealth can be held is in the form of money and bonds,
bonds being preferred because of the possibility of earning a
positive return. The stock of bonds is assumed proportional to
the stock of capital. The exact degree of proportionality is
unimportant. The crucial factor is that the stock of capital in
the economy should represent the existing accumulated wealth of
the economy and that increases in the stock of capital, amount
of wealth, have the effect of shifting the consumption function
upward. The consumption function is given by equation (5.5):

(5.5) $\qquad C = C(X,K)$

In the discussion which follows, it will be more convenient
to work with the savings function rather than the consumption
function. To illustrate briefly the savings function assumed,
suppose that the consumption function takes a linear form,
equation (5.6) where c_x and c_k represent the marginal propensity

(5.6) $\qquad C = c_x X + c_k K$

to consume out of real income and wealth respectively. Savings
are obtained by the definitional identity $S = X - C$ and are
given in equation (5.7) where s_x $(= 1 - c_x)$ is the marginal propen-

sity to save out of real income. If the savings function is drawn

$$(5.7) \qquad S = s_x X - c_k K \qquad s_x, c_k > 0$$

in the savings-output plane, an increase in the capital stock
will cause the savings function to shift to the right.

Real investment demand is a function of the actual rate
of real output, the existing stock of capital, factor prices,
and the state of technology. Equation (5.8) gives the investment

$$(5.8) \qquad I = I(X,K,W,R,T)$$

function. For given values of W, R, and T, the general shape of
the investment function is specified by Fig. 25, p. 108. Its
exact position in the investment-output plane will be determined
by the existing stock of capital.

Equations (5.1) and (5.3) jointly determine the actual
rate of output and the price level. The amount of labor demanded,
and thus employed, in the economy would then be given by equation(5.9)
which is simply the inverse of the short-run production function.

$$(5.9) \qquad L = L(X)$$

The model assumes that all labor demanded at the existing money
wage rate is supplied. This, of course, does not preclude movements in the labor market, although no specific equations to explain
the level of money wages will be given. Instead, it is assumed
merely that reductions in the rate of unemployment will have a
tendency to push money wage rates upward. If the ceiling of full-
employment should be encountered, the conclusions of the model

would, of course, have to be altered to take into account the now vertical aggregate supply curve.

Similarly, no precise equations will be offered to indicate the exact movement of interest rates. Instead it is simply assumed that a condition in which desired investment exceeds desired saving is likely to result eventually in an increase in interest rates. This increase will be amplified when and if the monetary authorities fail to satisfy the conditions of equation (5.4) and the growth in the supply of available funds is slowed. The opposite case of desired savings in excess of desired investment will tend to lower interest rates.

It would certainly be convenient if the equations of the present model could be specified explicitly and then solved to determine a rate of equilibrium growth for the system. The development of growth models along this line has done much to uncover the basic determinants of economic growth. From the original simple Harrod-Domar models, models of economic growth have become increasingly sophisticated. They have expanded to include multi-sector economies, monetary effects, international trade, expectations, and technical change.[1] All of these extensions

---

[1]Hahn and Matthews provide a survey of the literature in growth theory: "The Theory of Economic Growth: A Survey," Economic Journal, LXXIII (December, 1964). No attempt will be made to list all the growth models which have been developed; however, for examples of major works in this field see J.E.Stiglitz and H.Uzawa (eds.), Readings in the Modern Theory of Economic Growth (Cambridge: The M.I.T. Press, 1969); A. Sen (ed.), Growth Economics (Baltimore: Penguin Books, Inc., 1970); and K. Shell (ed.), Essays on the Theory of Optimal Economic Growth (Cambridge: The M.I.T. Press, 1967).

have been steps bringing the theory of economic growth closer to
reality. However, one assumption of these models still predominates in
economic growth studies and that is full-employment of the labor
force and the capital stock. Although it may be true that over
very long periods this assumption can be maintained to a degree,
it is certainly not valid for short-run movements in an economy.
Labor is not fully employed except in isolated periods, neither
is capital efficiently utilized at all times. The groundwork
provided by economic growth theory is useful for studying long-
term changes, but it provides little basis upon which a theory of
short-run movements can be constructed.

The Keynesian analysis has been useful in studying the
determination of output and employment in the short-run, but
it suffers in the context of growth since the capacity-generating
effects of investment are not explicitly considered. These capacity
effects have been built directly into the present study and this
may help to improve the applicability of Keynesian analysis to
growth. In the sections to follow, the equilibrium positions in
the economy implied by the savings (5.7) and investment (5.8)
functions will be first analyzed and then the comparative static
and the dynamic movements implied by parametric changes discussed.

Static Equilibrium Positions

The short-run equilibrium positions possible by combining
the savings and investment functions are illustrated in Fig. 26.
Depending on the precise value of the marginal propensity to save,
anywhere from one to five equilibrium positions will be possible.

The case of five possible equilibrium positions is illustrated in
Fig. 26 by the points A through E. Three of the equilibriums are
stable (points A, C, and E) while two represent unstable positions
(points B and D). This is in contrast to the earlier non-linear
investment function where there were two stable and one unstable
equilibrium positions. Like the investment function used by
Vanek there still exist a high "inflationary" equilibrium (point E)
and a low "depression" equilibrium (point A). Unlike the earlier
function, however, the economy need not be subject to a continuous
state of inflation or deflation nor need it, for that matter,
necessarily fluctuate between depression and boom periods. A
third stable equilibrium is provided by point C. By the nature
of the model, the equilibrium at point C represents what can be
termed an "optimal equilibrium" although no ethical considerations
are necessarily implied. The rate of output X_3 represents an
equilibrium rate of output, a rate at which desired investment
and savings are equal. X_3 can also represent an optimal rate
of output, a rate produced at minimum average cost with both
factors of production being paid their marginal products. The
unstable equilibriums serve primarily to mark critical rates of
output. If the actual rate of output, determined by the intersection of the aggregate supply and expenditure curves, should
fall below the rate X_2, a cumulative contractionary process would
begin pushing the economy toward the equilibrium represented by
the rate of output X_1. Similarly, an actual rate of output
exceeding the critical rate X_4 would lead to an expansion of

the economy to the stable equilibrium represented by X_5.

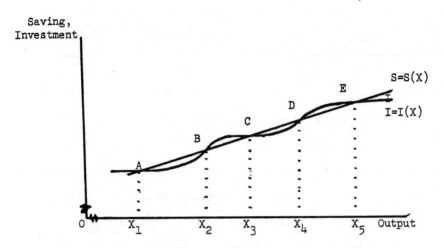

Fig. 26.--Possible short-run equilibrium positions
implied by the model.

The contraction to a state of depression with large
quantities of excess capacity or the expansion putting extreme
pressure on existing productive resources and leading to inflationary growth are not inevitable consequences of the model. It is
possible that the actual rate of output might fall somewhere
between the output rates indicated by X_2 and X_4. In this situation
the economy would move toward the equilibrium represented by X_3
which is characterized by the efficient utilization of existing
capital resources and low and stable price levels. Unfortunately,
the equilibrium represented by point C does not necessarily imply
efficient utilization of existing labor resources. Although the
labor being employed is being used most efficiently, it may be that
large amounts of labor are not being employed at all. This represents
a situation of disequilibrium in the labor market, a condition not

reflected in Fig. 26 except by the possible movements of the
money wage rate.

Long-Run Savings and Long-Run Investment Functions

Before going on to consider the effect of changing factor
prices or changes in technology, it will be useful to develop the
concepts of long-run savings and long-run investment. The long-
run savings function is the counterpart of the long-run consumption
function discussed in Chapter III. The long-run savings function
will be proportional to output, unlike the non-proportional short-
run version given in equation (5.7). To illustrate the interaction between the long-run and short-run savings functions, assume
that output has been increasing steadily. Producers in each
period correctly anticipate the increased demand and provide the
appropriate capital stock. With the increasing capital stock, the
savings function is continually shifting upward with the increased
stock of wealth. The path traced out over time under these conditions
would be similar to the long-run savings function obtained from
empirical studies. If the rate of output, for some reason, should
stop increasing and decline, the actual savings behavior of the
economy would be reflected by the short-run savings function. The
long-run and short-run savings functions are illustrated in Fig. 27.
Assume that initially the rate of output is X_1. The short-run
and long-run savings are identical and indicated by point A. As
output expands, the short-run savings function shifts upward along
LRS. Suppose output reaches a maximum rate of X_4 before it starts
to decline. Savings will now decline not along LRS, but along S_2.

Similarly, when output begins to expand again, savings will also expand, but along the short-run function S_2, until the rate of output X_4 is once more attained. At that point, the short-run function will begin shifting upward again.

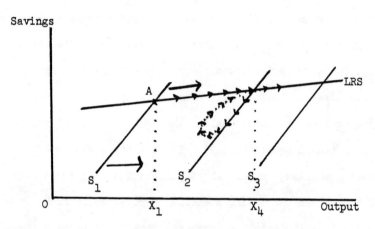

Fig. 27.--Long-run and short-run savings functions.

These considerations are tied to the behavior of the capital stock. Once output reaches a peak and then declines, there will be no further increases in capital since excess capacity will exist. In fact, the capital stock might also decline, which would cause the short-run function to shift back toward the left. However, the decline in capital stocks is limited by the rate of depreciation, and, in any case, will seldom ever exceed the rate of decline in real output. When output starts expanding again, excess capacity exists and there is no reason to expand the capital stock. The actual capital stock exceeds the desired capital stock, or, in terms of output, the actual rate of output is still less than the optimal rate of output. When the actual rate of output reaches and surpasses the optimal rate, investment expenditures will eventually lead to an expansion in the stock of capital. This expansion in the capital stock will then serve to start the savings function once more on its upward drift. The arrows in Fig. 27 indicate the probable direction of movements in savings as output expands to X_4, contracts just short of X_1, and then expands again up to and beyond X_4.

Just as a long-run savings function exists corresponding to the short-run savings function, so too can a long-run investment function be defined. Assume that the rate of output has remained steady at some given level long enough for the capital stock to adjust to its desired level. The long-run investment function would then specify the rate of gross investment appropriate to that rate of output. If the capital stock has had time to adjust to its desired level, that implies that the current rate of output is equal to the optimal rate of output. Thus the long-run investment function can be defined as the rate of gross investment for each rate of output, assuming that rate of output is the optimal rate. In the static analysis, the rate of gross investment when output was at the optimal rate was simply that rate of investment which served to maintain the existing productive capacity of the capital stock. In a dynamic context, the rate of gross investment appropriate when output is at the optimal rate might more appropriately be defined as that rate of gross investment which would not only maintain the existing productive capacity of the capital stock, but provide

also any additional output capacity anticipated by the normal
rate of growth in the economy. If the economy had grown over
the past several decades at, say, three per cent per year, then
in this context "normal" rate of growth would be three per cent.
These considerations will be pursued when the possibilities of
growth in the system are analyzed later in the chapter. For
the moment, the simpler static concept of long-run investment
function will be employed.

To illustrate the derivation of a long-run investment
schedule, assume that the production function takes the Cobb-
Douglas form. In Chapter II the relationship between the
desired stock of capital and the rate of output was calculated
for this case and given by equation (2.19) which is reproduced
below as equation (5.10). To relate long-run investment to the

$$(5.10) \qquad K^* = \frac{X}{A}\left(\frac{W}{R}\frac{\alpha}{\beta}\right)^{\beta}$$

rate of output, assume that the current rate of depreciation is
given by the parameter $\underline{u}$. Long-run investment is the rate of
depreciation times the desired capital stock at each rate of
output and is given by equation (5.11). This long-run investment

$$(5.11) \qquad LRI = u\,\frac{1}{A}\left(\frac{W}{R}\frac{\alpha}{\beta}\right)^{\beta} X$$

function is drawn with several short-run functions in Fig. 28.
The given stock of capital serves to determine the exact location
of the short-run function which is "anchored" on the LRI curve
by the position of central equilibrium. For example, investment
function I_1 indicates that the optimal rate of output for the

given stock of capital is X_1. Gross investment at a rate of
output X_1 will be just sufficient to maintain the existing
stock of capital. But this is precisely the rate of investment
indicated by the long-run investment function. As the capital
stock expands, the optimal rate of output will expand and the
short-run investment function will slide upward along the long-
run investment function.

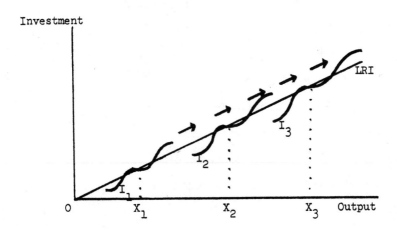

Fig. 28.--Long-run and short-run investment functions.

It remains to examine the relationship between the long-
run savings function and the long-run investment function. When
the two relations are graphed simultaneously, it readily becomes
apparent that the long-run average propensity to save and the
long-run average propensity to invest **cannot** vary too widely
from each other. Consider Fig. 29 where three possible long-run
investment functions are depicted for a given LRS: LRI(1) is
everywhere above LRS. In this situation, the desired rate of

savings is less than desired investment at all output rates above
X_o and, for output rates below X_o this disparity is maintained as
consumers travel down the short-run savings function, S_2.

It is clear that this situation cannot be maintained.
Desired investment continually exceeding desired saving will
generate considerable maladjustments within the system. In
particular, it might be expected that the rate of interest would
rise. A rise in interest rates, however, would change one of
the "constants" upon which the curves are drawn and cause them
to shift. The nature of the particular effects will be discussed
presently. Before that, however, consider LRI(3) in Fig. 29.
With this long-run investment function, desired investment would
continually be below desired saving. There would exist considerable
deflationary pressure in the economy and most likely a tendency
for the rate of interest to decrease. This situation, like the first,
is inherently unstable.

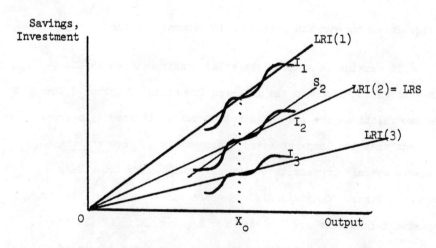

Fig. 29.--Long-run Investment and long-run savings functions.

The third possibility is that the LRI function be equal
to (or at least reasonably close to) the LRS function. In this
case, it is possible to attain an equilibrium rate of output for
the long and short-run functions simultaneously. Since most
economies seldom experience a continual state of depression or
a continual inflation, the most likely case appears to be the
present. Long-run investment would be expected to be reasonably
close to long-run savings. In fact, departures from this position
would eventually set into motion forces tending to correct the
disparity. To examine these forces, the parameters which have
been assumed constant up till now must be allowed to vary.

The Comparative Static Effect of Factor Price Changes

Since long-run consumption behavior has been relatively
stable, assume that any adjustment taking place will manifest
itself by a shift in the long-run investment curve. By taking
the derivative of (5.11), the comparative static properties of
this function can be obtained for the parameters involved in the
special case of a Cobb-Douglas production function. The results
are reproduced below. The first term indicates that the derivative
of the long-run investment function with respect to a change in
money wages is positive, i.e. an increase in money wages will ro-

$$(5.12) \qquad \frac{d(LRI)}{d(\ )} = \begin{array}{cccccc} W & R & \alpha & \beta & A & u \\ + & - & + & \pm & - & + \end{array}$$

tate the function upward. The first two effects are concerned
with factor-price movements and the remaining four with what can
be termed technological parameters.

For factor prices, an increase in money wages tends, as
noted above, to rotate the LRI curve upward. It might be useful
to consider the case of a wage increase in some detail, if only to
give an indication of how changes are likely to influence the
system. With respect to the price-output plane, the increase in
money wages will have two major effects: (a) the long-run average
cost of production will be shifted upward, and (b) the optimal
rate of output for the given stock of capital will decrease. With
no change in aggregate monetary expenditure, the result will be a
decrease in real output and an increase in the price level. The
situation is illustrated in Fig. 30. The optimal rate of output
has dropped to $X_{o'}$ from X_o and the long-run average cost curve has
increased from $LRAC_1$ to $LRAC_2$. If the rate of output were to be
maintained, there would be an increase in profits. However, with
a given amount of money expenditure and the shifting aggregate
supply curve, the rate of output will not be maintained and there
will be, in fact, no change in profits with a Cobb-Douglas function.

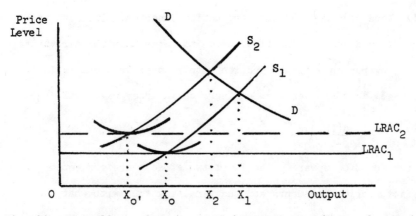

Fig. 30.--The effect of an increase in wages on prices and output.

Fig. 31 illustrates the effect on the profitability of
investment curve. The decrease in the optimal rate of output
means that for any rate of output above the optimal, the difference
between desired and actual capital stocks will be increased. The
profitability of investment, therefore, will increase for all
rates of output as the desired capital stock shifts to the right.
The costs associated with rapid capital acquisition, on the other
hand, do not depend directly on wage rates. The premium cost
curve remains unchanged.

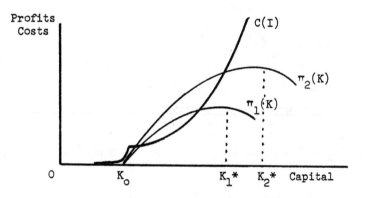

Fig. 31.--The effect of an increase in wages on the
profitability of investment.

The effect on the short-run investment function is
illustrated in Fig. 32. The rate of gross investment I_o was
sufficient to maintain the existing stock of capital at an output
rate of X_o. The change in money wages has made that given stock
of capital optimal for a lower rate of output, $X_{o'}$. The short-
run investment function has thus shifted to the left to the
position indicated by I_2. If the actual rate of output had been

X_o, the effect of the increased money wages would have been to increase

the desired rate of investment expenditures. Precisely how much

the rate of investment increases would depend on how large had

been the increase in money wages. If the capital stock were

correctly adjusted to an output rate of X_o under the new money

wage, the investment function would be I_2, which lies on the new,

higher, long-run investment function.

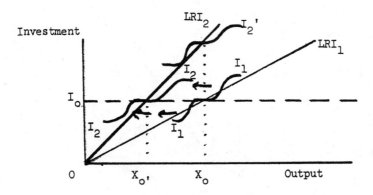

Fig. 32.--The effect of an increase in wages on investment.

A similar analysis of the effects of changing interest

rates can be undertaken but will not be discussed in detail. The

general effect of an increase in interest rates will be precisely

opposite to the increase in money wages: the long-run investment

function will shift downward. The present stock of capital becomes

optimal for a larger rate of output rather than a smaller. A drop

in interest rates has the same effect as an increase in money wages.

Note should be made here of the possibility mentioned in the pre-

vious section of a divergent LRS and LRI. The analysis above

indicates that if, during some short-run period, the LRI should be

shifted upward above the LRS function, the increase in investment
relative to savings, if it serves to increase the rate of interest,
will also serve to shift the LRI function back downward toward
the long-run savings function. This then reinforces the earlier
conclusion that the actual positions of LRS and LRI are likely
to be quite close to each other.

The Effect of Changing Technology

The effects of technological changes can be considered
here in very broad terms. The production function originally
introduced in Chapter II assumed a constant level of technology
which, of course, was a necessary assumption of the static analysis.
In a dynamic context, this assumption can be relaxed. Assume that
the production function takes the form of the Cobb-Douglas function
of (5.13) where K_e and L_e are capital and labor inputs measured

$$(5.13) \qquad X(t) = A(t)(K_e)^{\alpha}(L_e)^{\beta}$$

in "efficiency units" and defined by (5.14). This kind of

$$(5.14) \qquad K_e = K_o e^{at} , \qquad L_e = L_o e^{bt}$$

technological change assumes that the efficiency of the inputs
increases through time. Thus, one man-year of labor this year
might be equivalent to two man-years of labor a decade ago. On
this basis, there could be an increase in effective capacity each
period without any increase in the total absolute amount of
factor inputs employed. Capital, also would be measured in
efficiency units--one unit of capital today producing the equivalent of three units of capital of an earlier time period.

The term $A(t)$ reflects neutral shifts of the production isoquants, that is, both capital and labor share equally in the increase in efficiency. For the special case of the Cobb-Douglas production function a constant rate of growth of efficiency in factor inputs can be collapsed into the $A(t)$ term, thus making a separate analysis unnecessary--and empirically impossible. The capital and labor efficiency units are given by (5.14). Assume that the $A(t)$ term can be represented by (5.15). Substituting

$$(5.15) \qquad A(t) = A_o e^{ct}$$

equation (5.14) and (5.15) into (5.13) yields the expression (5.16)

$$(5.16) \qquad X(t) = A_o e^{ct} (K_o e^{at})^\alpha (L_o e^{bt})^\beta$$

which can be further reduced to (5.17), all three types of technical

$$(5.17) \qquad X(t) = A_o e^{\gamma t} K_o^\alpha L_o^\beta \qquad \text{where } \gamma = c + \alpha a + \beta b$$

progress represented in a new $A(t)$ term. It should be added that it is still possible to distinguish technological changes which affect the elasticity of output with respect to capital or labor.

The effect of an increase in A is to shift the LRI curve downward. This conclusion needs amplification. There are, in fact, two broad production function concepts relevant in the context of technological change and growth.[2] The first concept is that of the function which describes how the existing capital

---

[2] The analysis of the present section owes much to the work of W.E.G. Salter, Productivity and Technical Change (Cambridge: Cambridge University Press, 1969); see especially Chap. II: "Technical Knowledge and Best-Practice Techniques," pp. 13-26.

stock and the labor force can be combined to produce current real
output. Buried in this function are all levels of efficiency.
The actual stock of capital in an economy will be of varying ages,
or vintages, just as the productivity of individual workers varies
greatly. This production function describes how given resources
can best be used to produce current output. Another concept of
the production function, however, is possible. This function is
related to the current state of technology. It describes how
new capital, utilizing the current state of knowledge, can be
combined with labor to produce output. The economy, of course,
does not produce according to this function, but investment
decisions are based on it. The new function describes the productivity of new investment; the old function describes the actual
production in the economy. If capital equipment is being designed
so that it's efficiency increases by, say 10% per year, this does
not mean that the aggregate capital efficiency variable in (5.14)
above increases by 10 %. The actual increase in the K_e term, and
even more so the A term, is likely to be quite modest when
compared with actual technological advances occurring in the
economy. The reason is simply that it takes a considerably long
time before the current stock of capital can be replaced with
newer, more efficient capital.

The changing relationship between capital and output due
to technological changes can be reflected in the diagram of the
relationship between desired capital and output. In Fig. 33 (a)
the desired stock of capital is given as a function of the rate of

output and is represented by the line K = vX. If the capital

stock is K_0, optimal output will be X_0. Assume now that some

parametric change, for example an increase in money wage rates,

shifts the relationship between capital and output to the line

K = v'X. The optimal rate of output will become X_2. This is

because the change affects the entire stock of capital already

in existence. Similarly, changes in the elasticity of output

with respect to capital or labor which affect the current stock

of capital or current labor force will result in an optimal rate

of output of X_2.

Suppose, however, that the change in v to v' was the result

of an increase in technology embodied only in new capital equip-

ment. The new equipment will have a lower capital-output ratio

than current capital equipment. In this case, the output rate

X_2 would be optimal only if the entire stock of capital were

replaced by the new modern equipment. This, of course, is quite

unrealistic. Part of the capital stock will be replaced by the

new equipment, but not all of it. Assume a rate of depreciation

of u so that uK_0 capital units are needed for replacement. If

that amount is purchased of new equipment, the optimal rate of

output will be X_1 and the relationship between desired capital and

output will be given by the line OAB. With no other changes, de-

preciation of the older capital stock in the next period and its

replacement with the new, more efficient capital stock would move

the capital-output line to OA'B' and increase the optimal rate of

output to X_1'. It need not be assumed that the actual capital investment under these conditions will follow the above simplistic description. However, the change in the efficiency of new capital means that the depreciation of the old capital stock, uK_o, in Fig. 33 (a), results in a loss of productive capacity equal to X' but the addition of new capital equal to uK_o will increase productive capacity by more than X'. In fact, productive capacity would increase X" by the introduction of the new capital. Firms may not desire this much increase in productive capacity. They have the option of maintaining the existing rate of production and this can now be accomplished by a smaller investment expenditure than would have been required under the old technology. Which action is actually taken will depend on the capacity firms want to achieve through their investment expenditures.

One would expect the current stock of capital to display a whole host of varying capital-output ratios. In terms of productive capacity, with any fall in output the least productive capital would be the first idled. The relationship between current output rates and the desired capital stock based on current vintages is likely to look something like the curved line OA in Fig. 33 (b). The most efficient capital is that with the lowest capital-output ratio, represented by the line OB. Although new capital is clearly more efficient than older capital, it does not necessarily follow that it would pay to replace the old capital with the new equipment. Capital will, in general, be kept in production until it physically wears out, or it becomes economically obsolescent. By economical obsolescence is meant that it becomes cheaper to

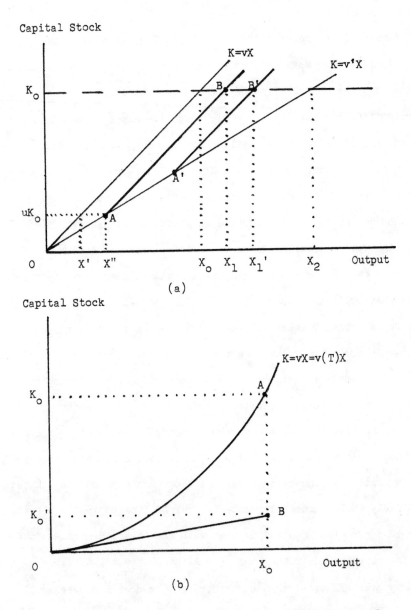

Fig. 33.--The relationship between the capital stock and
the optimal rate of output with different vintages of capital.

purchase new capital equipment entailing an additional capital
cost in addition to the necessary labor cost than it is to continue paying the current labor cost of older capital equipment.
Thus, when technological advances reduce the average cost of
production with new equipment below the marginal cost of production
of existing equipment, the existing equipment becomes technological-
ly obsolescent and it pays to invest in the new capital equipment.

The above kind of technological advance is not reflected
clearly in changes in the $\underline{A}$ term which measures technological
changes affecting the whole stratum of production, or new efficient
capital equipment which has been incorporated into the production
process. However, even in this very simple analysis, it can be
included in the discussion by means of the depreciation term $\underline{u}$.
If capital is normally wearing out at the rate of, say 5 % per
year, then investment for replacement of lost capacity will be
equal to 5 % of the existing stock of capital. Now, if a technological advance occurs which makes new equipment more economical
than some of the existing stock of capital before it has, in fact,
become physically obsolescent, then replacement investment in
that period must rise. The physical rate of depreciation has
been augmented by the increase in economically obsolescent
capital equipment. Thus, this kind of technological advance can
be reflected by an increase in the $\underline{u}$ term. The effect of this
on long-run investment is to shift the LRI function upward. The
optimal rate of output for the existing capital stock is calculated
only for the economical portion of the existing capital stock. A

technological change which renders some of this capital obsolete
will serve to reduce the optimal rate of output and thus intensify
any difference between actual and desired capital stocks if the
desired capital stock has been above the current stock. This
would increase investment expenditures. By the same token, if
the capital stock had been originally excessive, this would aid
in reducing excessive capital capacity.

The Possibilities of Economic Growth

Now that the various factors which cause a shift in the
LRI have been discussed, it remains to specify how the system
might react to growth in the economy. When the static analysis
is left to consider dynamic changes, the modification in the
definition of long-run investment discussed earlier becomes
necessary. The long-run investment function now reflects the
rate of gross investment, assuming that the capital stock is
adjusted to its desired level, required to provide the "normal"
expected increase in aggregate demand. Economic growth implies
that capacity, too, must expand. Producers would more reasonably
in this situation invest at a rate not only sufficient to maintain
the existing stock of equipment, but also sufficient to provide
the needed capacity for the output expected in the coming period.
The system remains in equilibrium if next period's output equals
the expected rate. It remains close to equilibrium if next
period's output is close to the capacity provided. Major changes
in investment plans are made only when output far exceeds or falls
short of predicted levels.

Fig. 34 illustrates some possible cases. Assume that the economy is initially at equilibrium at a rate of output X_o. The short-run savings and investment functions are given by I_o and S_o Equilibrium implies that the aggregate price level is near the point of minimum average cost. Under a system of steady growth, firms will have an expectation of next period's aggregate demand. If that expectation is a rate of output X_1, investment during the period will be sufficient to increase the capital stock to its new desired level. The process of net investment during the period will also serve to shift the savings function to the right since the wealth within the economy will be increasing. If the actual rate of output is X_1, producers' plans will be realized and they will continue in their normal investment behavior. However, actual output need not be exactly the expected output for firms to maintain investment plans. An actual rate of output anywhere between X_1' and X_1'' will be close enough to the expected rate to indicate that expectations are basically correct, or in any case, to indicate that they are not basically wrong. If, on the other hand, the actual rate of output exceeds X_1'', investment plans will be revised upwards, desired investment will exceed desired savings, and the usual multiplier process is likely to lead to a general expansion in output and income. Similarly, an actual rate of output below X_1' will lead to a reduction in investment plans. This, in turn, will cause a drop in aggregate demand and a cumulative contractionary process will begin. The system, of course, will not explode since stable equilibriums exist for both

the high and low rates of investment. In fact, it might be
possible for growth to occur at an extreme equilibrium position.
If an increase in aggregate demand causes an increase in desired
investment, the increased investment expenditures will themselves
lead to higher levels of aggregate demand. Investment will remain
high until capacity catches up with demand. The key question,
of course, is Will it? And, if capacity does catch up with demand,
what happens then? Can the economy maintain the high-level equilibrium position or must it eventually settle back into the normal
"optimal equilibrium" growth path? Under what conditions would
it sink into the depressionary equilibrium, and must the economy
stay there?

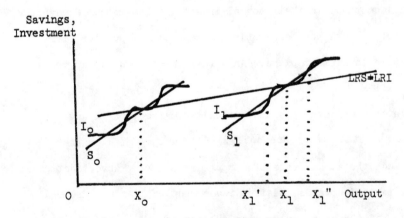

Fig. 34.--Possible outcomes in the process of economic growth.

The present model by itself will not indicate which is the
ultimate course of events. It indicates, rather, that many things
are possible. On the one hand, equilibrium growth at a relatively
constant price level is possible, provided only that investment

and spending plans are sufficiently correlated. Growth with
continually increasing prices is possible if the economy finds
itself trapped in the inflationary equilibrium. Under the conditions of the model, too many variables are assumed constant to
answer explicitly what will happen. As the economy moves in
one direction or another, some of the parameters which have been
assumed constant will, obviously, change. The change in the
parameters of the system will have the effect of shifting the
various functions. In this manner, the actual course of the
economy can be analyzed if only the appropriate assumptions are
made concerning the behavior of the parameters in the model. In
particular, the model allows, besides the possibility of continuous
growth, the probable occurrence of cyclical growth. Precisely
how the cycle is generated will depend upon the assumptions made
concerning the forces acting upon the economy. To illustrate
the flexibility of the present model as a framework in which the
possibility of cyclical growth can be discussed, the following
chapter discusses the leading theories of the trade cycle and
demonstrates how each can be explained employing the tools built
up in the present model.

Chapter VI

THE GENERATION OF CYCLICAL GROWTH

At the conclusion of Chapter V it was demonstrated that stable economic growth, either in an inflationary sense or in the optimal output sense, is conceivable in the present model. Cycles, however, are also possible. The exact behavior will depend on which of the parameters assumed constant are changed and in what order. The model developed in this study cannot be expected to reflect the exact working of an economy during any business cycle. It is too aggregative to take into account the many leads and lags and interrelationships occurring within a single business cycle. But some idea of the possible forces acting on the aggregative variables during a cycle can be gained. In this chapter, a number of previously developed theories of the business cycle will be examined to see whether the explanations they provide can be included within the framework of the present system. No attempt is made to cover all business cycles and those discussed are only sketched in brief outline.[1] The purpose is simply to see whether the present model

---

[1]The analysis of the present chapter owes much to the works of Haberler, Gordon, Lee, and Hansen. G. Haberler, Prosperity and Depression (Geneva: League of Nations, 1941) provides a more detailed analysis of various theories of the cycle. See, also, T. Wilson, Fluctuations in Income and Employment, third edition (London: Pittman, 1948), and A.H.Hansen, Business Cycles and National Income (New York: W. W. Norton, 1953). A shorter summary of business cycle theories

is, in fact, consistent with cyclical growth.

The Cycle Theory of W.C. Mitchell

Perhaps the most comprehensive explanation of cycles is that of Wesley C. Mitchell.[2] His approach is highly eclectic, including as it does many of the forces which other theorists point to as principal causes. However, there is one factor which Mitchell regards as of paramount importance in determining actual business activity, the profit motive:

> Every business establishment is supposed to aim primarily
> at making money. When the prospects of profits improve,
> business becomes more active. When these prospects grow
> darker, business becomes dull. Everything from rainfall
> to politics which affects business exerts its influence
> by affecting this crucial factor--the prospects of profits.[3]

Forces acting within a monetary, profit-seeking economy tend automatically to generate cycles and instability. These forces are found primarily in the continually changing price-cost relationships. To understand how they work, consider the normal sequence of events through a cycle.

After a time, a period of depression will produce conditions

---

is available in Lee, Macroeconomics: Fluctuations, Growth, and Stability (Homewood, Ill.: Irwin, 1971) and R. Gordon, Business Fluctuations (New York: Harber & Row, 1961), Chaps. 12 and 13, pp. 339-398.

[2]W. C. Mitchell, Business Cycles (Berkeley: University of California Press, 1913). For a shorter summary of Mitchell's position see his "Business Cycles," reprinted in American Economic Association (ed.), Readings in Business Cycle Theory (Homewood, Ill,: Richard D. Irwin, 1951), pp. 43-60.

[3]Mitchell, "Business Cycles," p. 45.

favorable to an expansion in business activity:

> Among these conditions are a level of prices low in comparison with the prices of prosperous times, drastic reductions in the cost of doing business, narrow margins of profit, ample bank reserves, and a conservative policy in capitalizing business enterprises and in granting credits.[4]

As the depression continues, costs are reduced and profit margins gradually improve, banks acquire excess reserves and become more willing to lend. Fig. 35 illustrates the state of the economy in a depression period. Assume the peak levels of demand had been D_1, but have since dropped to D_2. As a result price and output have fallen far below earlier levels. Profits are below their normal return and profit prospects are quite dim. In the process of disinvestment, or gradual adjustment of the optimal rate of output towards the lower current rate, the average cost curve will shift to the left. This will have the effect of reducing overhead costs. Prices will stabilize or start rising and the dismal profit picture will improve.

The availability of monetary resources will have a depressionary effect on interest rates, which will encourage investment. In addition, consumers will have depleted stocks of durable goods which sooner or later must be replaced. For one reason or another, therefore, demand begins to expand. With a given supply curve, this will result in time in an increase in prices:

---

[4]_Ibid._, p. 47.

While the price level is often sagging slowly when a
revival begins, the cumulative expansion in the physical
volume of trade presently stops the fall and starts a
rise. For when enterprises have in sight as much business
as they can handle with their existing facilities of
standard efficiency, they stand out for higher prices on
additional orders.[5]

In terms of Fig. 35, the depression has brought the optimal rate
of output closer to the actual rate. In the process, the actual
rate of output begins to expand because of expansions in aggregate
demand. This expansion results in an increase in the price level
and in profits. The combined effect of current profits and
expanding output leads to expectations of further output increases
which increase the rate of investment. Increasing investment
then itself adds to the level of aggregate demand and a cumulative
process is underway.

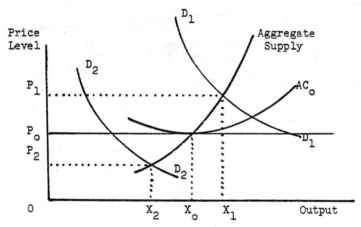

Fig. 35.--Movements in prices and production from the boom
period to the depressionary period.

---

[5]Ibid., p. 48.

In Mitchell's analysis, the process of expansion must come
to an eventual halt because of stresses built up in the system as
expansion progresses.

> Among these stresses is the gradual increase in the
> costs of doing business. The decline in overhead costs
> per unit of output ceases when enterprises have once
> secured all the business they can handle with their
> standard equipment, and a slow increase of these costs
> begins when the expiration of old contracts makes neces-
> sary renewals at the high rates of interest, rent, and
> salaries which prevail in prosperity. Meanwhile the
> operating costs rise at a relatively rapid rate. Equip-
> ment which is antiquated and plants which are ill located
> or otherwise work at some disadvantage are brought into
> operation. The price of labor rises, not only because
> the standard rates of wages go up, but also because of
> the prevalence of higher pay for overtime. More serious
> still is the fact that the efficiency of labor declines,
> because overtime brings weariness, because of the employ-
> ment of "undesirables," and because crews cannot be driven
> at top speed when jobs are more numerous than men to fill
> them....A second stress is the accumulating tension of the
> investment and money markets. The supply of funds available
> at the old rates of interest for the purchase of bonds,
> for lending on mortgages, and the like, fails to keep pace
> with the rapidly swelling demand. It becomes difficult
> to negotiate new issues of securities except on onerous
> terms, and men of affairs complain of the "scarcity of
> capital." Nor does the supply of bank loans grow fast
> enough to keep up with the demand. For the supply is
> limited by the reserves which bankers hold against their
> expanding liabilities.[6]

The first stress Mitchell discusses is nothing more than

the operation of the law of diminishing returns. As output expands,

more labor is hired for the fixed capital stock, output expands,

but marginal costs increase. The expansion in output moves the

actual rate from the optimal to a rate exceeding the optimal rate,

---

[6]Ibid., pp. 50-51.

thus average costs are also rising. Mitchell assumes more than
simply these phenomena, however. In the process of the upswing,
labor money wage rates increase as more of the existing supply of
labor is hired. The effect of this is to shift the aggregate
supply curve to the left and to increase minimum average costs.
Similarly, when replacement of capital is undertaken, the new
capital must be financed at higher interest rates. This has a
two-fold effect in the analysis. The substitution of more
expensive fixed capital costs for a part of the capital stock
will serve to augment the already rising minimum average cost
curve. The increase in interest will serve to diminish the
desired stock of capital for any rate of output and hence reduce
investment expenditures. Monetary effects mentioned by Mitchell
work in this same direction in that they aggravate the increase
in interest rates. They also have another effect. If the supply
of funds becomes limited because of a decrease in excess reserves,
then the monetary authorities can no longer supply the necessary
monetary resources needed to effect the real aggregate demand
desired. As a result, the growth in the aggregate expenditure
curve will be limited.

Mitchell envisions two ways in which actual capital catches
up with desired capital. One has just been mentioned in the
forces restricting monetary growth. Another is found in the
limits of physical production encountered at full-employment:

> The credit expansion, which is one of the most regular
> concomitants of an intense boom, gives an appearance of
> enhanced prosperity to business. But this appearance is

> delusive. For when the industrial army is already
> working its equipment at full capacity, further borrowings
> by men who wish to increase their own businesses cannot
> increase appreciably the total output of goods. The
> borrowers bid up still higher the prices of commodities
> and services, and so cause a further expansion in the
> pecuniary volume of trade. But they produce no correspond-
> ing increase in the physical volume of things men consume.[7]

This would be reflected in the aggregate supply curve becoming

vertical when full-employment of labor is encountered. Since

real output cannot expand, or can expand only at the rate of the

increase in the labor force, actual capacity catches up with

desired capacity.

The combined effect of increasing wages, increasing

interest rates, and limited increases in monetary expenditure

results in a narrowing of profits and a much more rapid dis-

appearance of insufficient capital stock. As the desired capital

stock is brought near the actual capital stock, investment expendi-

tures slow down. This further intensifies problems by reducing

aggregate monetary expenditure at the same time that capacity

is still expanding. With a decline in profit margins, creditors

refuse new loans and seek repayment of old debts. A process of

liquidation begins, money is contracted and real investment demand

decreases resulting in a rapid drop in aggregate demand. As a

result, the economy now finds itself with considerable excess

capacity, low rates of output, low prices, and low to negative

profits, and in a depressionary state at which our analysis of

Mitchell's theory began.

Although Mitchell's analysis stresses largely cost-push

relations and neglects the "real" factors underlying these
movements, nevertheless his arguments can be summarized in terms
of the savings and investment diagrams developed here. In
Fig. 36 assume that the economy is in a boom period. Actual real
output is X_1 while the optimal output is X_o. Output, employment,
investment, and prices are all relatively high. The high investment leads to increasing capacity--X_o will be shifting to the
right--and also to increasing demand: the fact that desired
investment exceeds desired saving at X_1 indicates an upward
pressure on real output. In Mitchell's analysis, the capacity
catches up with that demand for a number of reasons. Increasing
interest rates shift the LRI function downward and serve to
reduce the discrepancy between actual and desired capital--also
reducing the degree of excess demand in the economy. Aggregate
monetary demand may be limited by a restriction in monetary
expansion. In this case, increases in money wage rates and
interest costs in the face of a stabilized rate of aggregate
expenditure will serve to lower both current and potential
profits. In Fig. 36, this implies that, in spite of the excess
real demand, the limitation of available money resources will
keep the actual rate of real output from expanding. Limitations
of available resources in the productive sector will also, in
time, restrict the increase of real output--if full-employment
of labor is encountered, there can be no further increases in
real output no matter what the increases in aggregate expenditure.
As the above forces bring the actual stock of capital rapidly in
line with the desired stock, investment expenditures begin to

decline. However, the decline in real demand when capital is now near the desired level, results in an excess of capital which then further aggregates declining investments. The decline in investments, and perhaps also a decline in monetary stocks, leads to major reductions in the level of aggregate demand and hence aggregate expenditure and the economy finds itself in a depression. This depression is then corrected by a combination of real and monetary forces which tend to move actual and desired capital stocks once more closer together. In real terms, depreciation reduces the actual stock of capital, and a gradual lowering of interest rates increases the desired capital stock. When the two become sufficiently close to entail an increase in investment, aggregate demand increases and the whole process starts anew.

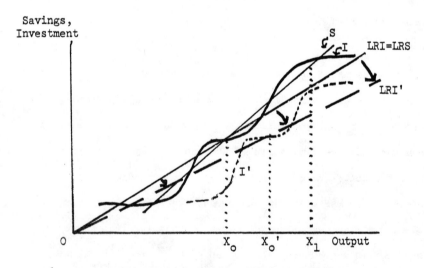

Fig. 36.--The interaction of savings and investment as optimal capacity catches up with actual output rates.

Psychological Theories of the Cycle

The discussion of business cycles began with Mitchell
because many of the other theories which place predominant
importance on specific aspects of the cycle are included in
his over-all analysis. For example, a group of theorists
have placed a great deal of emphasis on psychological considerations as the main determinant of business cycles. Mitchell
attaches a certain importance to psychological factors, but
does not make them the cornerstone of his theory. Writers
in this category include Keynes, Pigou, Beveridge, Lavington,
and Taussig.[8] Gordon provides an apt summary of the position
taken by this shcool:

> When an expansion begins for any reason, errors of
> optimism are inevitably generated, not merely in a few
> industries but through the entire economy. Business
> optimism improves not only in proportion to the improve-
> ment in the underlying "real" factors but more rapidly
> than this. In planning ahead, businessmen overestimate
> future demand and underestimate the future rise in costs.
> Such optimistic errors are especially likely in invest-
> ment projects that will yield consumers' goods only in
> the relatively distant future.... For a while, this
> growing optimism feeds on itself. Finally, after a
> "period of gestation," an increased supply of goods
> comes on the market. Businessmen find that their rosy

---

[8] J.M.Keynes, The General Theory of Employment, Interest
and Money, chap. 22, (New York: Harcourt, Brace & World, Inc.,
1964); A.C.Pigou, Industrial Fluctuation (London: Macmillan &
Co., Ltd.,1927), chaps. 6-7; W.H.Beveridge, Unemployment: A
Problem of Industry (London: Longmans, Green & Col, Inc., 1909);
Lavington, The Trade Cycle: An Account of the Causes Producing
Rhythmical Changes in the Activity of Business (London, 1922);
Taussig, Principles of Economics (second edition; New York: The
Macmillan Co., 1916).

anticipations were unwarranted. A revulsion sets in, and the psychological pendulum now swings to the opposite extreme. Disappointment now breeds errors of pessimism; the pessimism feeds on itself and generates a cumulative downswing. Eventually, businessmen find that their pessimism has gone too far; some profitable opportunities remain and others eventually develop; the pessimism gradually dissipates; and a new psychological cycle begins.[9]

As Haberler has pointed out, if the psychological theories meant nothing more than that, during the upswing people are optimistic and during the downswing pessimistic thus resulting in more investment in the upswing and less in the downswing, they would add nothing more to the present analysis.[10] On definite economic "real factors," the investment function developed in Chapter IV indicates that high investment rates are to be expected in the upswing. But the psychological theories say more than this. They imply that the optimism goes beyond the level indicated by real factors.

> When demand and prices have continued for a while to rise, people get into a habit of expecting more and more confidently a further rise of equal or approximately equal extent--that is to say, they project current experience too confidently into the future.[11]

The psychological theories thus have their major impact on expectations. In terms of the investment function, the fact that the economy has been advancing, that desired investment has exceeded desired saving, lessens the reluctance of firms to regard minor increases as permanent. The marginal propensity to

---

[9]Gordon, op. cit., pp.347-48.

[10]Haberler, op. cit., p. 145.   [11]Ibid., p. 148.

invest becomes more sensitive to increases in output. Or,
in other words, the critical rates of output surrounding the
central optimal equilibrium position, shrink toward the optimal
rate and even small increases in the rate of real output become
sufficient to set the economy climbing toward the high inflationary equilibrium. Carried to its extreme, the narrowing of the
region of low marginal investment propensities in the neighborhood of the optimal rate of investment would reduce the investment function to the non-linear Vanek function; only two equilibriums would then be stable: inflation or depression.

For the excessive optimism to turn to excessive pessimism,
the psychological theory needs an additional assumption and that
is that current rates of investment expand capacity only with a
lag. In a boom period, when both prices and output rise in
response to increased demand, firms cannot be sure what real
aggregate demand for their product is. It is quite possible that
each firm will read the high level of prices and profits as
indicating a much larger share of the market for the firm if
only it can expand its capacity. If many firms react in this
manner, when the capital stock is finally installed actual
capacity suddenly becomes more than required by current demand.
This disappointment is immediately magnified into a pessimistic
view of the future, i.e., any small decreases in the rate of
output imply a permanent decrease, and the contraction is
under way.

Over-Investment Theories of the Business Cycle

A number of theorists have sought the explanation of cycles directly in the savings-investment mechanism. These theories emphasizing investment behavior have several points in common: (1) the impetus to fluctuations derives from the inherent instability of long-run investment; (2) the volume of investment rises to a level which it is impossible to sustain; and (3) the eventual decline in the rate of investment sets off a cumulative contraction. All three points are compatible with the model developed here. The theories differ in their explanation of the turning points, the reason why investment eventually turns down. They have been called cumulatively "over-investment" theories since all assume that the boom period is characterized by a disequilibrium of the capital stock. A rate of investment is undertaken which is high enough to set off the boom, but which at the same time also initiates forces which eventually result in its decline.

Monetary Theories. The over-investment theories can be broken into two broad classifications: monetary and nonmonetary. The monetary over-investment theory is represented primarily in the writings of F. A. Hayek.[12] Hayek's argument deals with the disequilibrium generated between the consumption and investment

---

[12]F.A.Hayek, Monetary Theory and the Trade Cycle (New York: Harcourt, Brace & Co., Inc., 1933); Prices and Production (London: George Routledge and Sons, Ltd., 1935); Profits, Interest and Investment (London: George Routledge and Sons, Ltd., 1939).

goods industries. Since the present model contains only a
single sector, this aspect of his theory cannot be discussed.
However, other points made by Hayek can be usefully analyzed
for a single sector economy. Hayek, building on the foundations
laid by Wicksell,[13] distinguishes between a market rate of
interest and a "natural" or "equilibrium" rate. This
equilibrium rate has been defined by Gordon "as the rate of
interest at which the demand for loanable funds just absorbs
the current flow of savings."[14] In terms of our model, then,
the natural rate of interest is that rate which makes the long-
run investment function identical to the long-run savings
function. In a depression, Hayek claims that the market rate
of interest falls below the natural rate (the long-run investment function rotates upward above the long-run savings function),
resulting in an increase in desired capital and, hence, increased
investment. The rise in desired investment above current savings
results in a disequilibrium position. Hayek assumes that it is
primarily the banking system which satisfies the increased demand for funds through the extension of bank credit. The result
is that the investment goods industry can now bid goods and
resources away from the consumer goods industry, resulting in a
rise in prices and money income. In the context of this model,

[13]Wicksell's position can be found in his Lectures on
Political Economy (London: Routledge and Kegan Paul, 1934).

[14]Gordon, op. cit., p. 358, ff. 32.

any expansion of bank credit need not lead to an immediate rise in prices if the stock of capital is above the desired stock. In fact, with considerable excess capacity, aggregate demand can expand even if financed by the creation of new money, without any immediate increase in the aggregate price level.

During the boom, the desired rate of investment exceeds the desired rate of saving. The expansion of credit allows the discrepancy to continue for a time, but sooner or later, the expansion in credit slows or stops altogether. Now the high rate of desired investment cannot be financed except with available savings. The result will be an increase in interest rates, declining investment, and the start of the downswing.

Non-Monetary Theories. The non-monetary theories of the over-investment school are somewhat similar to Hayek's, although much less emphasis is placed on the effect of bank credit. The principal economists in this group are Professors Spiethoff and Cassel.[15] Below, Hansen summarizes Cassel's theory of the cycle. It will be apparent that it fits readily into the present model if the terms "fixed capital goods" and "capitalized value of fixed capital goods" are replaced with the concepts of capital, K, and desired capital, K*, employed here:

---

[15]Spiethoff's position can be found in "Krisen," Handworterbuch der Staatswissenchaften, fourth edition, Vol. 6, 1925, pp. 8-91; this has been translated into English in an abridged form: "Business Cycles," International Economic Papers, no. 3, pp. 75-171; G. Cassel, Theory of Social Economy (New York: Harcourt, Brace & Co., Inc., 1923).

The cycle is due to lags in the responses of entrepreneurs to a society which is experiencing new outlets
for fixed capital investment--outlets caused by (a) inventions, (b) industrialization of undeveloped areas,
and (c) growth of population. These outlets raise the
value of fixed capital goods above their cost. Now the
lags enter the picture. In the boom, interest rates
rise and the cost of construction of new fixed capital
goods rises. The anticipated annual returns in fixed
capital are now capitalized at a higher rate of interest,
and thus the capitalized value of fixed capital goods
falls. On the other side, the cost of construction of
new capital goods rises. The combined effect of these
two developments is to cut the margin between value of
capital goods and cost of capital goods eventually to
zero. The inducement to invest in new fixed capital
goods therefore is destroyed. Investment falls off and
so do output, income, and employment. In the depression,
the rate of interest falls and so the value of fixed
capital rises, while at the same time the cost of construction of new capital goods falls. Thus the value of new
capital goods is now high in relation to cost, and so
the inducement to invest is restored.[16]

The boom is thus ended by a combination of rising

interest rates and rising prices for the capital good which

together serve to reduce the desired stock of capital, bringing

desired and actual stocks rapidly close together. The cycle

described above would, in time, die out if not for the

"recurring boosts given by inventions, territorial expansion

and population growth to the value of fixed capital goods."[17]

In fact, a whole class of authors has given inventions and

innovations the major role in determining both growth and cycles.

These theorists will be discussed in a later section.

---

[16]Hansen and Clemence, op. cit., p. 116.

[17]Ibid., p. 117.

Multiplier-Accelerator Mechanisms

Economists who emphasize over-investment note the
critical importance of investment and capital movements. The
major force, however, which controls investment movements is
assumed to come from changes in interest rates or a departure
between market and natural rates of interest. As has been
shown, these assumptions can be incorporated into the present
model which deals with investment as a function of the rate of
income, albeit a very complex function. The more recent
approach to cycle theory has emphasized the relation between
income movements and capital changes as the primary determinant
of cycles. These theories are Keynesian in spirit, relying
on interactions between consumption, investment, and income.
They all rely on the fact that investment produces not only an
increase in capacity, but also an increase in income through the
multiplier. They can be termed "capital-stock adjustment theories"
since investment occurs primarily as an adjustment of the capital
stock to changing output conditions. The main difference in
these theories lies in the way investment is assumed to react
in response to changing income. In fact, the model developed
in this paper can be included in this class, relying as it does
on income movements, as well as factor prices, technology and
present capacity, to determine investment.

The heart of these models is found in the multiplier-
accelerator model.[18] Consumption is taken as dependent on

-----

[18] P.A.Samuelson, "Interactions between the Multiplier

157

income.[19] Investment is a function of the difference between
income last period and the income of the period before that. The
factor of proportionality, $\bar{v}$, is the accelerator which can be
interpreted as a technological relationship between increases
in output and the necessary increases in capital required to
produce this extra output. Stated here in its simplest form,
the model can be specified by equations (6.1) through (6.4):

(6.1) $\qquad C_t = cX_t$

(6.2) $\qquad I_t = \bar{v}(X_{t-1} - X_{t-2})$

(6.3) $\qquad X_t = C_t + I_t$

(6.4) $\qquad X_t - (\bar{v}/s)X_{t-1} + (\bar{v}/s)X_{t-2} = 0$

Equation (6.4) expresses the interaction of the multiplier,
the inverse of the marginal propensity to save, and the
accelerator. The introduction of lags into the process has
resulted in a difference equation of second order. More
complicated models have produced equations of even higher
order. When a difference, or differential, equation of
second-order (or higher) is solved, the resulting growth path

Analysis and the Principle of Acceleration," <u>Review</u> of <u>Economics</u>
and <u>Statistics</u>, XXI (May, 1939), pp. 75-78.

[19]Consumption in (6.1) is assumed a function of current
income ; however, lags have been introduced into this relationship.
The critical property of the multiplier-accelerator models is
found in the solution (6.4) which becomes a second-order difference
equation.

can be either steadily expanding or falling, cyclically damped or explosive.[20] Which path will predominate depends on the values of the parameters involved.

As a theory of investment, the accelerator principle suffers on many counts.[21] It assumes a rigid connection between changes in output and changes in investment given by the constant capital-output ratio, $\bar{v}$. The present model also specifies a capital-output ratio, but it is conceptually far different from that envisioned in the accelerator principle. The relationship is strictly between the rate of output and the desired capital stock, not the actual capital stock. In addition, this relationship is subject to change whenever any of the underlying factors such as technology or factor prices which determine it change. Even if a strict technological relationship between capital and output were assumed to exist,

---

[20] For an excellent discussion of the basic properties of difference and differential equations see A.C.Chiang, Fundamental Methods of Mathematical Economics (New York: McGraw-Hill, 1967), chaps. 14-17, pp. 423-571.

[21] For a summary of some of the earlier literature on the acceleration principle see Haberler, op. cit. pp. 85-105. A more recent critical evaluation is found in A.D.Knox, "The Acceleration Principle and the Theory of Investment: A Survey," Economica, XIX (August, 1952), pp. 269-297, reprinted in E. Shapiro, (ed.), Macroeconomics: Selected Readings (New York: Harcourt, Brace & World, Inc., 1970), pp. 49-74. The criticisms voiced in the present section are based largely on Knox's analysis. For further criticisms of the acceleration principle see S.C.Tsiang, "Accelerator, Theory of the Firm, and the Business Cycle," Quarterly Journal of Economics, LXV (August, 1951), pp. 325-341; R.S.Eckaus, "The Acceleration Principle Reconsidered," Quarterly Journal of Economics, LXVII (May, 1953), pp. 209-230; G.H.Fisher, "A Survey of the Theory of Induced Investment," Quarterly Journal of Economics, LXVI (April, 1952), pp. 474-494.

the accelerator would only be operative in cases of "full-capacity" output. Although the authors who write of the acceleration principle recognize this fact, few in fact define the concept meant by "full-capacity."[22] The operation of the accelerator must be asymmetrical between periods of economic growth and periods when real output is declining. A sharp decline in output would call forth a similar sharp decline in investment, but the decline in investment will be limited by the rate of depreciation.[23] The acceleration principle considers net investment when, for reasons mentioned earlier, gross investment is preferable. And finally, the expectation hypothesis assumed in the acceleration principle is quite naive since it states that entrepreneurs always expect current output to be maintained into the coming period:

> The supposition which underlies the rigid application of the acceleration principle is that the level of demand is assumed to rule in the future also. Now it is very doubtful whether it is possible to generalize as to the exact behavior of producers in this respect. Fortunately for the broad result, however, it is sufficient to indicate a certain range of expectations as probable and to eliminate others as highly unlikely.[24]

Despite the analytical difficulties of employing the accelerator as a theory of investment, the basic interaction of the multiplier and the accelerator can be useful in discussing

---

[22]Knox, op.cit., p. 56.

[23]J. Tinbergen, "Statistical Evidence on the Acceleration Principle," Economica, V (1938), p. 165.

[24]Haberler, op. cit., p. 343.

cyclical movements. The theories which are based on the interaction of these two forces can be divided into two broad groups
on the basis of their treatment of the specific investment function. On the one hand, the cycle is explained by employing the
strict accelerator model and adding assumptions about other
exogenous forces; on the other, a theory of the cycle is developed
which allows investment to be much more loosely coordinated with
changes in output and income.

Hicks' Theory of the Trade Cycle

Hicks has developed perhaps the best-known of the specifically accelerator models.[25] Hicks' model uses the basic multiplier-
accelerator framework in which the parameters imply explosive
cyclical growth. By adding appropriate assumptions about a
"ceiling" on the maximum rate of output and a "floor" on the
minimum rate of output, the cycle is kept within reasonable
bounds. Hicks manages to incorporate growth into the system by
assuming given autonomous investment expenditures growing at a
constant rate. Hicks' model does not fit well into the present
framework. Although both models employ a concept of the capital-
output ratio, in the present system the determinant of investment
spending is based not on the change in the rate of real output,

---

[25] J.R.Hicks, A Contribution to the Theory of the Trade Cycle,
(London: Oxford University Press, 1950). For critiques of Hicks'
model see S.S.Alexander, "Issues of Business Cycle Theory Raised
by Mr. Hicks," American Economic Review, XLI (December, 1951),
pp. 861-878; J. Duesenberry, "Hicks on the Trade Cycle," Quarterly
Journal of Economics, LXIV (August, 1950), pp. 464-476; and A.Burns,
Frontiers of Economic Knowledge; Essays, National Bureau of Economic
Research (Princeton: princeton University Press, 1954).

but rather on the change in real output relative to the optimal
rate of output and is dependent upon the given technology, and
factor prices. Without a rigidly defined investment pattern,
the development of explosive cyclical growth is no longer a by-
product of the system.

Goodwin's Non-linear Accelerator

A much more flexible application of the accelerator is
provided by Richard Goodwin.[26] Goodwin's model is based on what
he terms the non-linear accelerator and comes closer to the spirit
in which the present model has been derived. "Net investment is
undertaken as long as the desired capital is greater than existing
capital, and disinvestment in the contrary case."[27] Goodwin
assumes that desired capital is determined jointly by the acceleration coefficient, v, and an additional function B(t) which reflects
technological change, (6.5). Even if the technological term is

$$(6.5) \qquad K* = vX + B(t)$$

---

[26]See R.M.Goodwin, "The Nonlinear Accelerator and the
Persistence of Business Cycles," Econometrica, XIX (January, 1951),
pp. 11-17; "Secular and Cyclical Aspects of the Multiplier and the
Accelerator," Income, Employment and Public Policy: Essays in
Honor of Alvin H. Hansen, (New York: Norton, 1948); "A Model of
Cyclical Growth," The Business Cycle in the Post-War World, Erik
Lundberg, (ed.), (London: Macmillan & Co. Ltd.,1955), pp.203-221,
reprinted in American Economic Association, Readings in Business
Cycles (Homewood, Ill.: Richard D. Irwin, Inc.,1965), pp.6-22.
R.G.D.Allen, Macro-economic Theory (New York: St.Martin's Press,
1968) provides a mathematical interpretation of Goodwin's model,
pp. 374-383. The notation here differs from Goodwin's.

[27]Goodwin, op. cit., (1955), p. 210.

ignored, equation (6.5) is not the strict acceleration principle since it relates desired, and not actual, capital to output. Goodwin's assumptions on this point follow those developed here "it is assumed here that with a given stock of capital we can produce more (by overtime, etc.) then it was designed to produce, and, obviously, also less. Furthermove, in designed capacity, there is usually some stand-by or peak-load capacity which can be used."[28]

Investment is given as a function of the difference between desired and actual capital stocks:

(6.6) $I = I(K* - K)$

The actual function, however, is nonlinear:

> For the sake of simplicity, we assume that the pressure to expand is proportional to the difference between (K*) and (K), subject to two crucial non-linearities. The lower one is set by the rate of wastage of capital at zero gross investment, and the upper one by the maximum output of new capital goods obtainable with given capital and labor supply.[29]

Investment as a function of the difference between desired and actual capital stocks is illustrated in Fig. 37(a). L represents the upper limit on net investment and M the lower limit on dis-investment. By extending the analysis to include a nonlinear accelerator in the central portion and by introducing lags, the investment function is smoothed out to the dotted line in Fig. 37(a). It is interesting that the above function, translated into a

---

[28]Ibid., p. 211.   [29]Ibid.

relation between the rate of output and gross investment, takes
on an appearance quite similar to the Kaldor and Vanek functions
discussed in Chapter IV. This conversion is illustrated in
Fig. 37(b). The actual working of the Goodwin model to produce
cycles is aptly summarized by Gordon:

> Once output begins to rise after a depression, the stock
> of capital desired by businessmen will rise; and hence
> investment will increase, thus increasing income, output,
> and the desired capital stock still further. Eventually,
> investment can rise no further because the capacity of the
> capital goods industries is limited. Once investment
> stops increasing, (or increases only very slowly as the
> industries producing capital goods gradually expand their
> capacity), income will stop rising. This will stabilize
> the desired stock of capital, except as it is further
> increased through innovations. The actual stock of
> capital keeps on increasing, however, because of the large
> amount of investment currently being made. Eventually,
> the actual stock of capital catches up with that which
> businessmen want to have; investment then declines; this
> pushes down income, which lowers the desired stock of
> capital; and a cumulative contraction gets under way.[30]

Goodwin's explanation of the cycle thus corresponds to the
explanation given by Kaldor. Kaldor assumes a nonlinear savings
and a nonlinear investment function. Since there is little
evidence that the savings function is nonlinear as assumed by
Kaldor, and since his conclusions hold even if it is linear, the
savings function will be assumed linear in this study. When the
nonlinear investment and the savings functions are joined, there
are three equilibriums with the equilibriums at the high and low
levels of activity the stable positions (see Fig. 21, p. 96).

---

[30]Gordon, op. cit., pp. 375-6.

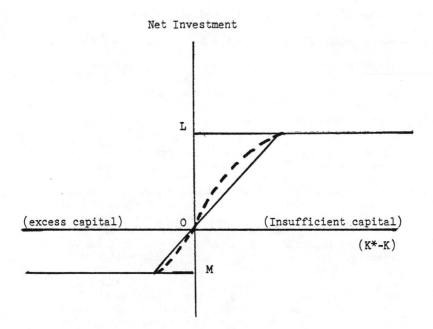

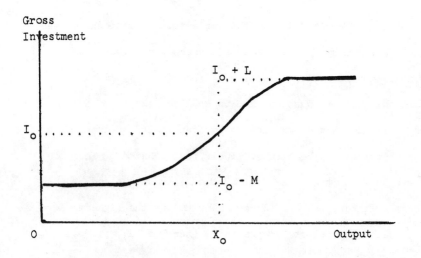

Fig. 37.--Goodwin"s nonlinear accelerator and the implied
investment function.

Kaldor finds the key to the trade cycle in the fact that the
savings and investment functions determining these positions are
short-run functions which set into motion forces that eventually
make the stable equilibrium positions unstable. In the high
activity equilibrium, investment levels are high and the capital
stock, as it increases, shifts the investment function toward the
right. After a time, it will shift beyond the savings function
yielding only the lower equilibrium as a possible solution. With
investment at the level described by the lower equilibrium, the
investment function gradually shifts to the left until once more
the low equilibrium becomes unstable and the economy expands
toward the high income levels. This explanation of the cycle
is disturbed by the present model incorporating as it does a
stable central equilibrium.

Duesenberry's Theory of the Cycle

A still more flexible approach to the relationship between
investment and output has been adopted by James Duesenberry.[31]
Investment is regarded simply as an unidentified function of
capital and output (6.7). The exact nature of the function

$$(6.7) \qquad I = I(K,X)$$

will depend on the values of the exogenous variables in the system.

---

[31] *Business Cycles and Economic Growth* (New York: McGraw-Hill,
1958), Chaps. 9,10. A somewhat similar model can be found in
A. Smithies, "Economic Fluctuations and Growth," *Econometrica*,
XXV (January, 1957), pp. 1-52.

In building his model, Duesenberry divides investment expenditures into two classifications, business investment and housing investment. Business investment is specified by equation (6.8) and housing investment by (6.9), where Y, K_b, K_h, E, π, D, and R are personal disposable income, business capital stock, stock of houses, retained earnings of business, profits, business debt, and capital-consumption allowances respectively. By a number of

$$(6.8) \qquad I_{bt} = F(Y_{t-1}, K_{bt-1}, E_{t-1}, \pi_{t-1}, D_{t-1}, R_{t-1})$$

$$(6.9) \qquad I_{ht} = F(Y_{t-1}, K_{ht-1})$$

simplifying assumptions, Duesenberry modifies the above investment formulations into a simpler investment function which is made to depend on lagged output, capital stock, and profits, and current capital consumption allowances. The latter two variables, however, are functions of output and capital. The final investment function, then takes the form of (6.7) above. By assuming linear functions, Duesenberry's model is reduced to the following four equations:

$$(6.10) \qquad I_t = \alpha Y_{t-1} + \beta K_{t-1}$$

$$(6.11) \qquad C_t = a Y_{t-1} + b K_{t-1}$$

$$(6.12) \qquad K_t = (1-u) K_{t-1} + I_t$$

$$(6.13) \qquad Y_t = C_t + I_t$$

If equation (6.10) is regarded as a linear approximation of the present investment function, Duesenberry's model would be identical to that developed here: investment is gross investment, consumption depends on income and the capital stock, and investment

is a function of income and capital. (The effects of profits and
various costs of capital acquisition would be buried in the α and
β parameters.) The model given in equations (6.10) to (6.13)
can be reduced to a single equation in the variable Y:[32]

(6.14) $Y_t = (\alpha+a)+(\beta+1-u) \; Y_{t-1} + \alpha(\beta+b)-(\alpha+a)(\beta+1-u) \; Y_{t-2}$

The result is, again, a second-order difference equation
similar to that derived in the simple multiplier-accelerator
model. However, the above parameters provide a system much more
stable than the simple multiplier-accelerator system. In fact,
the normal operation of Duesenberry's model leads to steady growth.
Duesenberry relies on a variety of disturbances to explain the
booms and depressions of real life: fluctuations in autonomous
investment, speculation, monetary disturbances, etc. Since the
present investment function is only poorly represented by a linear
approximation, Duesenberry's conclusions can not be adopted for
this analysis. However, since the model does come very close to
the present, it is interesting that it derives a conclusion which
allows steady growth while at the same time admitting cycles due
to various exogenous shocks.

Schumpeter's Theory of the Cycle

Technological change is one of the shocks which Duesenberry
would have regarded as important. Recall that the over-investment
theories of Cassel and Spiethoff also relied on shocks brought

---

[32]Ibid., p. 197.

about by such factors as technical change, the opening of new
markets, or population growth. A number of theorists have placed
heavy reliance on these shocks, explaining both the process of
growth and cycles as functions of technological progress. The
leading exponent of the importance of innovations is undoubtedly
Joseph Schumpeter, although similar positions are held by Hansen
and by Robertson.[33] In developing his innovation theory, Schumpeter,
of course, recognizes other factors which affect actual cycles
and which differ from one cycle to another:

> The individual setting of most of the great crises in
> history is more important for the explanation of the
> actual happenings observed in each case than anything
> which enters into a general theory--supposing such a
> theory to be possible--which can therefore never be
> expected to yield more than a contribution to either
> diagnosis or remedial policy in any actual case.[34]

In spite of all the forces, both external and internal, which
affect the economic system and produce actual cycles, the fact
remains that cycles as such have pervaded economic life since
the beginnings of the capitalist era. In order, then, to search
for a key element unlocking the entire cyclical pattern, Schumpeter

---

[33]J.A.Schumpeter, The Theory of Economic Development (New
York: Oxford University Press, 1961), esp. Chap. 6; and Business
Cycles (New York: McGraw-Hill, 1939); "The Explanation of the
Business Cycle," Economica, (December, 1927); and "The Analysis
of Economic Change," reprinted in American Economic Association,
Readings, pp. 1-19 from Review of Economics and Statistics, XVII
(May, 1935), pp. 2-10. A.H.Hansen, Fiscal Policy and Business
Cycles (New York: Norton, 1941), Chaps. 1,11-12,14,16. D.H.Robert-
son, A Study of Industrial Fluctuation (London: P.S.King & Son,
Ltd., 1915).

[34]Schumpeter, op. cit., (1961), p. 222.

assumes the absence of all other forces in the system making for
instability. In describing his theory of innovations, that
assumption will be adopted here also.

With the problem thus formulated, the question remains,
why is it that economic development has proceeded in fits and
starts rather than in a smooth continuous sequence? Schumpeter's
answer is short and precise:

> ...exclusively because the new combinations are not, as
> one would expect according to general principles of
> probability, evenly distributed through time--in such
> a way that equal intervals of time could be chosen, in
> each of which the carrying out of one new combination
> would fall--but appear, if at all, discontinuously in
> groups or swarms. Italics original .35

Sketched briefly, Schumpeter's argument would be something
like this. From an initial equilibrium position, sooner or later,
the advance of technology (or the opening of new markets or a
new form of market organization or a new source of raw materials)
opens up the prospect of profitable investment by the adoption
of the new technique. Leading entrepreneurs see the opportunity
and undertake the new investment, usually financed through the
creation of new money by the banks. Once the new investment is
begun, aggregate demand is increased, resulting, in the short-run,
in an increase in prices and output. The increase in aggregate
demand then spurs other sectors of the economy to increase their
investment expenditures and the boom is underway.

When the new investment has been completed, the new products

35Ibid., p. 223.

start to pour out onto the markets just as investment expenditures
are slowing down due to the drying up of innovative possibilities.
The original loans are now paid back, but this only serves to
reduce total credit and restrict further aggregate demand. A pain-
ful process of adjustment to the new production techniques takes
place as prices drop and production contracts. Since the boom is
usually characterized by speculative excesses, the process of
decline goes beyond the correct equilibrium position for the
economy. The depression is regarded as a period of adjustment
to the new conditions and the economy gradually approaches the
stable equilibrium incorporating the new innovations. Of course,
once the equilibrium is finally attained, the economy is ripe for
another disturbance from yet another series of technological
innovations.

Schumpeter elaborates his theory more carefully, but
hopefully the above sketch isolates its essential elements. The
process of growth described by Schumpeter can be explained within
the context of the model developed in this study. Schumpeter
emphasized that innovations come in swarms. Innovations are,
properly speaking, the implementation of various inventions.
Critics of Schumpeter have found it difficult to see any particular
reason for the inventive process to be so bunched. But they lose
sight of the distinction between invention and innovation. It is
entirely possible that invention proceeds quite smoothly, in fact,
that assumption shall be adopted here. In the present model,
technological changes which affect the entire stock of capital or

the entire labor force are incorporated in the parameter $A(t)$.
However, the vast majority of technological changes require some
form of investment.

This kind of change can be viewed as changing the rate of
depreciation. For example, if the actual capital-output ratio in
the economy is 2, with an existing capital stock of 1,000 units,
output will be 500 units. Suppose now that depreciation of the
physical stock of capital goods is 10% per period. 100 units of
capital, capable of producing 50 units of output, will wear out
each period. If a technological change makes the capital-output
ratio of new investment goods smaller than two, say 1.98, then
100 units of new capital would produce 51 units of output. The
remaining 449 units could now be producing with an existing capital
stock of 898 units. As a result of the technological change,
therefore, 100 units of the present stock have physically worn
out while 2 units have economically worn out. In this sense, then,
the technological advance can be regarded as a change in the actual
rate of depreciation.

Consider Fig. 38. An increase in the rate of depreciation
rotates the long-run investment curve upwards. Assume that the
economy is initially in the equilibrium position indicated by
point A. Since all other forces have been assumed inoperative,
point A represents a static equilibrium with desired investment
equal to desired savings for both the short- and the long-run
functions. The gradual improvement in technology slowly shifts
the LRI curve upward. Given the nature of investment, however,

this has initially no appreciable effect on investment. It slowly reduces the optimal rate of output in comparison with the actual rate at X_o, but given the flat section of the investment curve, investment plans remain unaltered. Eventually though, the distance between the optimal and actual rate of output will exceed the critical distance and an increase in investment expenditures becomes warranted. At this stage, some businessmen increase investment expenditures and start incorporating the new techniques. The increase in investment increases aggregate demand which then further increases investment and the normal business expansion is underway. Investment will attain a maximum level and so too will aggregate output, say at a rate X_2. The installation of the new equipment must move the optimal rate of output upward, in fact, certainly beyond the original optimal rate of X_o or it would not have represented an improvement in the first place. Assume that the new technique eventually moves the optimal rate of output up to X_1.

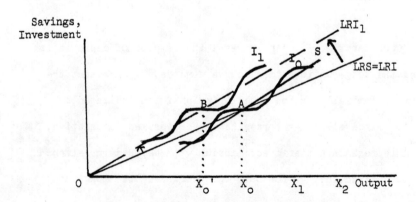

Fig. 38.--The accumulation of inventions leading to Schumpeter's "swarms" of investments.

For an explanation of the downturn and the resultant depression, consider Fig. 39. During the upswing of the boom, a
number of forces have been operating to shift the long-run investment function back downward. The slow effect of technological
change served to shift the function to the left. The installation
of new equipment and its incorporation into the current productive
process has exactly the opposite effect: it increases the productivity
of the current operating capital stock, an increase in the parameter
A, which shifts the long-run function downward. In fact, it would
be expected that the downward shift of A would outweigh the slow
upward shift due to the development of new techniques. Assume
technology is advanced at the rate of 1 % per period. The analysis
has just shown how a number of periods will be required to make
the installation of new inventions worthwhile. Thus, after for
example six periods, the new capital will represent a 6% improvement over existing techniques. When the degree of improvement
reaches some critical level, innovation becomes worthwhile. The
process of innovation will incorporate the latest techniques and
a certain portion of the capital stock will be replaced with new
equipment which is considerably more productive than the old.
As a result, the increase in A during the period when the equipment is installed and becomes operative is likely to far outweigh
the slow gradual improvement shown by the parameter u. In addition,
when the new capacity is installed and starts producing output,
the loans originally made to finance the investment are repaid.
The result is a simultaneous increase in output and decrease in

credit. As the boom progresses, it is also expected that interest
rates would rise. The effect of rising interest rates complements
the installation of new equipment in shifting the long-run investment function downward. With the LRI shifting downward and capacity
gradually increasing, a point will inevitably be reached when the
short-run investment falls below long-run savings. This occurs
at an optimal output of X_1 in Fig. 39, with the economy experiencing
an actual rate of output of X_2.

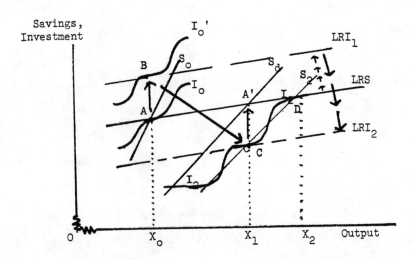

Fig. 39.--The expansionary and contractionary process
of Schumpeter's theory.

As a result of the above forces, the economy has reached
its peak and output now starts its downward adjustment. In the
downswing of the cycle, there will be forces operative which will
start the long-run investment function back towards the long-run
savings function. Once the new equipment has been installed, the
downward shift due to the A factor will be stopped while the con-

tinual slow increase due to the steady stream of inventions continues. As the depression continues, interest rates will begin
to decline; this shifts the LRI upward. Another factor which may
be of importance is the increase in wages which usually continues
after the economy has reached a peak in production. Increasing
wages will hasten the upward shift of the LRI curve.

In Schumpeter's analysis, the process of adjustment to the
new equilibrium usually goes too far. In Fig. 39, from the initial
equilibrium at point A, the short-run investment function gradually
shifted upward as the accumulation of new inventions shifted the
LRI function upward, until it reached the point B. At this stage
desired investment everywhere exceeded desired savings and the expansion was under way. As expansion continued, the increased investment would increase both the capacity and the wealth in the economy.
The increased wealth effect would cause the short-run savings function to shift upward along the LRS along with the expansion in output. For the short-run investment function, the increase in the
capital stock would cause it to shift to the right, the increase
in efficiency, to shift down. The net result would be a movement in the south-easterly direction toward the point C. As
capacity expanded, eventually the desired investment would catch
up with and fall below the desired savings. With desired savings
now exceeding desired investment (point D), the contraction would
begin. Initially, there would be very little depreciation of the
new capital stock; savings would move downward with the decrease
in output along the short-run savings function. At the same time,

the LRI would, due to the forces mentioned previously, start shifting back upward. The final equilibrium could be attained at the point A' where the system would be ready for another expansionary phase.

The above is how the analysis might be carried out if outside extraneous forces could be ignored. However, their effect on the individual cycle under consideration need not produce the above result with the economy settling at the center equilibrium, although this is the result Schumpeter considered the "normal" course of events:

> The economic picture of a _normal_ period of depression ...is throughout not so black as the mood pervading it would lead one to suspect. Apart from the fact that a great part of economic life remains almost untouched as a rule, the physical volume of total transactions in most cases falls only insignificantly. How exaggerated the popular conceptions of the ravages caused by a depression are, is shown by any official investigation of crises.... This is true not only of analysis in terms of goods but also of that in terms of money, in spite of the fact that the cyclical movement, with its inflation in prosperity and deflation in depression, must be especially strongly marked in the money expression. Total incomes rise in the boom and fall in the depression not more than 8 to 12 per cent as compared with the figures for average years, even in America (Mitchell), where the intensity of development presumably makes the fluctuations more strongly marked than in Europe. Aftalion has already shown that the fall in prices during depression only constitutes a low percentage on the average, and that really great fluctuations have their causes in the special conditions of the individual articles and have little to do with the cyclical movement. The same thing may be shown for all really large general movements, as for example the post-war period. When the phenomena of the abnormal course of events (panics, epidemics of bankruptcies, and so forth), which are continually becoming weaker, and with them anxiety about incalculable danger, disappear, public opinion will also judge of depressions differently.[36]

---

[36]_Ibid._, p. 246.

That such abnormal conditions can lead to prolonged depression is apparent in Fig. 39. If the crisis is marked by a financial panic and a sharp decline in money and credit, it is quite likely that the rate of output will fall so fast that it will not be caught by the center equilibrium. This consideration is reinforced if the money stock is viewed as part of the stock of wealth. In this case, the rapid decrease in monetary assets will cause the short-run savings function to shift to the left--an outcome which makes the possibility of the economy ending in the central equilibrium position more remote. Instead, there will be a continual drop in income, output, and employment until the depression equilibrium is reached. It is significant in this context to note that since 1909, the most severe recessions or depressions in the American economy, 1920-21, 1929-33, and 1937-38 were preceeded and accompanied by the most severe monetary contractions.[37]

Monetary Theories of the Cycle

The importance of money to cyclical movements brings the discussion to the last major group of cyclical theorists.[38] Money

---

[37] B.W.Sprinkel, Money and Markets, A Monetarist View (Homewood, Ill.: Richard D. Irwin, Inc.,1971), p. 113.

[38] There are, in fact, two other major groups of cycle theory which have been omitted from the present survey since they have few modern adherents. One is the "underconsumption" theories represented in the writings of W.T.Foster and W.Catchings: Money (Boston: Houghton Mifflin Co., 1923); Profits (Boston: Houghton Mifflin Co.,1925); and The Road to Plenty (Boston: Houghton Mifflin Co., 1928). Another major group of theorists attach importance to such factors as the weather and agriculture. For a review of these

is considered last in this brief review not because it is any less important than the other theories. Rather, the recent revival of interest in monetary effects indicates that it is likely to be of crucial importance. Certainly, most of the writers reviewed above would attach importance to monetary movements. Many, in fact, incorporate money changes into their theories to help explain various phases of the cycle. The position of the monetary cycle theories, however, goes beyond these earlier theories in assuming that monetary movements, rather than reflecting changes brought about by interactions of the several real phenomena involved, actually cause the cycle.

This position was maintained early in this century by Hawtrey and can be found also in the writings of Warburton and, most recently, Milton Friedman.[39] This explanation places the originating impulse

theories see Haberler, op. cit., Chap. 7, pp. 151-67.

[39]Hawtrey's position can be found in his Good and Bad Trade (London: Constable & Co., Ltd., 1913); Currency and Credit (London: Longmans, Green & Co., Inc., 1928); Monetary Reconstruction (New York: Longmans, Green & Co., Inc., 1926); The Art of Central Banking (London: Longmans, Green & Co., Inc., 1933); and Capital and Employment (London: Longmans, Green & Co., Inc., 1937).

Although Warburton did not state an explicit theory of the cycle, his position can be found in the papers reprinted in C. Warburton, Depression, Inflation, and Monetary Policy: Selected Papers, 1945-1953, (Baltimore: Johns Hopkins, 1966), see in particular Part I: The Role of Money in Business Fluctuations.

For a discussion of the possible mechanism by which money causes cyclical changes see M. Friedman and A.J. Schwartz, "Money and Business Cycles," Review of Economics and Statistics, Supplement XLV (February, 1963). Other works giving his views on the relation between money and stability can be found in the following: "The Demand for Money: Some Theoretical and Empirical Results," Journal of Political Economy, LXVII (August, 1959), pp. 327-351; "A

to cycles with the monetary authorities. An increase in the supply of money leads immediately to an increase in aggregate demand through the relation of MV to the rate of aggregate expenditure. The increase in aggregate expenditure may come directly if the banks make loans to firms and allow investment to exceed current savings, or indirectly, if the banks buy securities, depressing interest rates and thus stimulating investment. The collapse is explained by the opposite movement; a constriction of the money supply.

It is clear how this explanation can be included in the present model. Throughout, it has been assumed that any increase in aggregate demand indicated by the movement of the variables within the system could be affected. This implies that the monetary authorities increase the supply of money as needed. The results will be quite different if they do not. If desired investment should exceed desired saving, and if the banks do not increase the current stock of money, then the only way the excess investment can be financed is through the current monetary resources of firms in the economy. This implies a change in velocity. The change in velocity, however, is generally only a temporary phenomenon

---

Monetary and Fiscal Framework for Economic Stability," _American Economic Review_, XXXVIII (June, 1968), pp. 245-64; "The Supply of Money and Change in Prices and Output," _The Relationship of Prices to Economic Stability and Growth_, Compendium, U.S. Congress Joint Economic Committee Document No. 23734, March 31, 1958 (Washington, D.C.: U.S. Government Printing Office, 1958), pp. 241-56; and "The Lag in Effect of Monetary Policy," _Journal of Political Economy_, LXIX (October, 1961).

as the community adjusts to the restriction of monetary supplies. The increased rate of expenditure cannot be maintained with the given stock of money. What will most likely happen is that interest rates will rise as firms compete with each other for the limited funds until an equilibrium is reached between desired savings and investment.

Although it seems obvious that monetary restriction can act as a major deterrant to growth, it is not quite as clear that expanding monetary policy, say in the form of an increase in excess reserves, will necessarily lead to an expansion in aggregate demand. The point is currently under extensive debate and will not be pursued here. The position will be taken, rather, that monetary restrictions can affect the workings of the system and when appropriate, should be included in the analysis.

The present chapter has attempted to demonstrate how the various cycle theories could be explained using the tools of the present model. This, of course, is in anticipation of applying the framework to an analysis of the events leading up to 1929. Before that is attempted, however, some perspective must be acquired. In particular, how did the major parameters of the model behave prior to and during the 1920's? In the following chapter, a brief sketch of the major technological movements which occured in the years following 1899 is presented. The explanation of the observed acceleration in technology will most likely be found hidden in these technological and institutional changes.

Chapter VII

TECHNOLOGICAL PROGRESS IN THE EARLY TWENTIETH CENTURY

Introduction

The years which ushered in the 20th century have generally been regarded as a transitionary period in American history.[1] During this time the nation slowly awoke from the quiet ease of rural 19th century America to the exciting and complicated tempo of a modern urban economy. This transitionary character of the Progressive Era has been stressed by Walt Rostow.[2] America had come to the end of its drive to industrial maturity. Ahead lay the age of high-level mass consumption. The interim period, from the turn of the century into the decade of the 1920's, takes on increased significance when the discussion of Chapter I is recalled, for somewhere in this intriguing period of American history lies the secret of the acceleration in technical progress. It is not the purpose of this chapter, however, to chronicle the events which characterized the movement of the economy during this period; that task has been performed quite adequately elsewhere.[3] Rather, an

---

[1] H.S. Commager, The American Mind (New Haven: Yale University Press, 1950), pp. 41 ff.

[2] W.W. Rostow, The Stages of Economic Growth (New York: Cambridge University Press, 1960), pp. 73-74.

[3] For an interesting survey of the first half of the twentieth century see F.L. Allen, The Big Change: America Transforms Itself, 1900-1950 (New York: Harper & Row, 1952). The first two decades of

attempt will be made to sketch in very broad strokes the out-
lines of technological progress during the period. Although the
entire development of the economy is extremely complicated, the
major types of technological change can be isolated and incorporated into the model developed in earlier chapters. This will
then allow an examination of the theoretical implications of this
acceleration in technology for the aggregate variables of the
national economy.

Technological progress is often pictured as a new labor-
saving machine capable of vastly increasing current output rates.
Well, this certainly does happen, but the total picture is much
more complicated. Improvements in production can come from improvements in labor as well as capital inputs. The very process
of production can be the vehicle of change through improved
organizational methods, changes in market structure leading to
economies of scale, or improvements in the distribution of output.
Very often the process of technological change feeds upon itself,
an improvement in one industry making possible further advances
in other industries--an almost inevitable outcome when improvements originate in the capital goods industries or industries producing intermediate products. In addition to explicit production

the period are treated in Faulkner, The Decline of Laissez Faire,
1897-1917 (New York: Holt, Rinehart and Winston, 1951). The
decade of the 1920's is covered by F.L.Allen, Only Yesterday,
(New York: Harper & Row, 1964); G. Soule, Prosperity Decade:
From War to Depression, 1917-1929 (New York: Harper & Row, 1968);
and W.E.Leuchtenberg, The Perils of Prosperity, 1919-1932
(Chicago: University of Chicago Press, 1958).

and organizational changes, institutional changes quite often
accompany, if they do not necessarily precede, major innovational
advances. Such areas as consumer attitudes, government policies,
financial structures are all important in this respect. In the
present chapter these various facets of technological progress will
be examined as they pertain to the period under consideration.

Mechanical Innovations

This, like many other periods in American history, saw the
introduction of a whole host of labor-saving machines. To cite
only a few examples,

> New glass machines reduced labor time 97 per cent in the
> production of electric bulbs...cigar machines reduced
> labor between 50 and 60 per cent; a warp-tying machine
> in textiles dispensed with ten or fifteen workers for
> each machine; new machines in clothing shops reduced
> pressing labor between 50 and 60 per cent; in mixing
> mills of automobile tire plants labor per unit was re-
> duced about one half by the Banbury mixer; a new method
> of making inner tubes increased output per man about
> four times.[4]

Even unskilled labor was eliminated by such inventions as mechanical
loading devices in the mining of bituminous coal, where 25 to 50 per
cent of loading labor was eliminated, and the finishing machine for
cement highways, which eliminated from 40 to 60 per cent of the
labor on finishing.[5]

---

[4]Soule, op. cit., p. 129. For a more extensive discussion
see H. Jerome, Mechanization in Industry (New York: National
Bureau of Economic Research, 1934).

[5]Soule, op. cit., p. 129.

The list of specific inventions could easily be extended, but these are only manifestations of a technological revolution more basic than any single machine would imply. The true innovations of the period are found in the introduction of entirely new products; inventions which produced not merely a new machine, but a new industry. Leaders in this regard are undoubtedly electric light and power, chemicals, and, of course, the automobile. It was primarily these three, Schumpeter believed, that carried the long wave of economic development in the Kondratieff which developed after 1897.[6] It was these three industries which provided the foundation upon which many of the later inventions were based. Each will be examined in turn.

Leading Sectors of Growth

The Development of Electric Power. The inventions necessary to large-scale expansion in the electric power industry were already available by 1899. Thomas Edison had constructed the first central power station in New York, both alternating current and a reliable AC motor were available, and the steam turbine had been perfected. These developments made possible the generation of electricity at a low cost. With low-cost electrical power available, municipalities began the conversion from gas to electric lighting and industry gradually replaced other forms of power with electric power. Between 1899 and 1919 the percentage of industrial power

---

[6]J.A.Schumpeter, Business Cycles (New York: McGraw-Hill Book Co., 1929), I, p. 415.

supplied by electric motors increased from 1.8 per cent to 31.7
per cent;[7] by 1929 the output of the electric utilities had
increased fifty times over that of 1899[8] and industry was now
some 70 per cent electrified.[9] A huge amount of capital was
required as the electric utility industry expanded; capital in
the industry increased from $83,660,000 to $857,855,000;[10] by
1919 capital in the industry was over ten times its value in
1899. Labor, on the other hand, increased only five-fold during
the period, expanding from 42,013 in 1899 to 212,374 in 1919.
The development of electric power was of crucial importance to
the advancement of industry. By providing a new and efficient
means of power, it opened up a new era of innovational possibilities
enabling almost every industry in the economy to benefit.

The Chemical Industry. The chemical industry experienced
a rapid rate of growth during these years. From an index of
output of 18.3 in 1899, output increased to an index of 100.0
in 1929, an increase of 438 per cent.[12] Although the industry did

---

[7]Faulkner, op. cit., p. 124

[8]J.W.Kendrick, Productivity Trends in the United States
(Princeton: Princeton University Press, 1961) Table H-VI,p. 590.

[9]E.C.Kirkland, A History of American Economic Life (New
York: F.S.Crofts & Co., 1940), p. 645.

[10]Faulkner, op. cit., p. 127.

[11]The development of cheap electric power provided not only
a new source of power for industry, but made possible the growth
of another important industry during this period: rapid transit in
the form of street railways.

[12]Kendrick, op. cit., Table D-IV, p. 471.

benefit greatly by the take-over of thousands of German patents
in the dyestuffs industry after World War I, considerable progress
had been made before this. The expansion of the Solvay process
and the development of the electrolytic process following the
availability of cheap electric power were major boosts in the
production of the basic alkalis. Heavy chemicals such as sul-
phuric acid, ammonia, and the alkalis showed substantial progress
during this period. These, in turn, led to advances in the industries which utilized the chemicals. Another feature of extreme
importance was the development of synthetics by the chemical
industry. Here were materials which could not only reproduce
nature, but could provide products superior to nature's. Examples
which readily come to mind are rayon, artifical rubber, and the
seeds from which the plastics industry grew, celluloid and bakelite. Chemical discoveries such as these led to the creation of
vast industries which provided new and more efficient products for
the industrial machine.

The Automobile. Perhaps no other invention has had as
profound an effect on the life of the nation as the introduction
of the automobile. In the short span of just twenty years the
automobile had changed from "a picture of the arrogance of wealth"
to a practical necessity of every household.[13] The rank of auto-

---

[13] Of 123 working class families interviewed in 1923, 60
of them had cars. Of these 60, 26 lived "in such shabby-looking
houses that the investigators thought to ask whether they had
bathtubs, and discovered that as many as 21 of the 26 had none.
The automobile came even before the tub!" Allen, op.cit., (1964), p.136

mobiles in terms of the value of products in American industry
records its amazing rise: 150th in 1899, 77th in 1904, 21st in
1909, 7th in 1914, 2nd in 1919, and by 1925 it reached first
place.[14] There are a number of reasons for this phenomenal
growth, not the least of which is Ford's adoption of the assembly-
line principle, which illustrated to the entire world what Frederick
Lewis Allen has called the "dynamic logic of mass production." In
modern terms, Ford demonstrated the possibilities of economies of
scale in manufacturing. With each expansion in the production of
the Model T, the price declined: from $950 in 1909-1910 to $780,
$690, $550, $490, $440, $360, to finally, in 1924, the amazingly
low $290.[15] The continual lowering of price made possible the
purchase of automobiles by the great mass of consumers, a necessary
prerequisite to mass production. Of course, the expansion of the
automobile industry was accompanied by many major technical innovations such as electric starters, electric headlights, demount-
able rim tires, closed rather than open cars, and balloon tires to
mention but a few. But the crucial innovation was the wholesale
adoption of assembly-line production. This method of production
itself led to other practices such as the standardization of parts

---

[14]A.D.Chandler, Jr., Giant Enterprise, Ford, General Motors
and the Automobile Industry (New York: Harcourt, Brace and World,
1964), p. 5. For more detailed studies of the rise of autos see
A.Nevins and F.E.Hill, Ford; The Times, The Man, The Company (New
York: Scribner's, 1954), Vol. I; R.C.Epstein, The Automobile
Industry (Chicago: A.W.Shaw Co., 1928).

[15]Allen, Big Change, pp. 100-101.

(spark plugs, wheel rims, screw heads, etc.) so crucial to mass production techniques.

The impact of the automobile industries' growth extended far beyond the industry itself. The technical demands of the auto industry during these years virtually revolutionized the machine tool industry which "hummed with the whirl of the new engine and turret lathes, automatic screw machines, vertical millers, and radial drills and resounded with the sound of the monster stamping machines."[16] The new products of the auto industry required not only new tools but also new and improved raw materials as well. The metal and metal-working industries responded: high-speed carbon tool steel, which more than doubled the productivity of machine tools, was introduced by Bethlehem Steel. Hession and Sardy note other improvements:

> After 1910, molybdenum, tantalum, and tungsten-steel alloys were produced by the steel companies. Improvements in the metallurgy of copper, aluminum and other non-ferrous methals were leading in these same years to increased efficiency in their use in the automobile and other industries of the nation.[17]

These innovations, of course, served to feed back upon the auto industry itself increasing productivity there even more. Table III records the gain in productivity experienced by the industry through the period. While actual production increased two thousand times

---

[16] C.H.Hession and H.Sardy, Ascent to Affluence, A History of American Economic Development (Boston: Allyn and Bacon,1969), p.559.

[17] Ibid., p. 561.

the production in 1899, the output per man-hour increased just
under thirteen times its 1899 rate with much of this increase
coming in the years following the war.

TABLE III

OUTPUT AND LABOR PRODUCTIVITY IN THE MOTOR VEHICLE AND
EQUIPMENT INDUSTRY, 1899-1929.
(1929=100)

Item Year:	1899	1909	1919	1929
Output	0.05	1.8	28.2	100.0
% increase		3,500	1,467	254
Output/Man-Hour	7.8	8.3	33.0	100.0
% increase		6	298	203

Adapted from J.W.Kendrick, Productivity Trends in the
United States (Princeton: Princeton University Press,1961),p.482.

The growth in automobiles had a major impact on the various
industries which supplied the raw materials of auto production.
Rubber products increased over 2,000 per cent between 1899 and
1929; petroleum and coal products showed a 435 per cent increase;
steel mill products, 325 per cent; and glass 300 per cent.[18] Not
only those industries which supplied raw materials directly, but also
all those which eventually sprung up to serve the needs of the new
mobile public benefited. As Soule has pointed out, the industry

...reinforced the demand for good roads and inaugurated

---

[18]Kendrick, op. cit., Tables D-IV, pp. 467-475 and D-VI,
pp. 483-487.

an era of road builiding that enlarged public expenditures
and continually stimulated expansion. It facilitated the
growth of metropolitan regions at their outskirts by the
building of suburbs, and thus was interlocked with the
housing boom. It provided expanding markets for the petroleum industry, and caused a rash of filling stations, hot-
dog stands, cabin camps, and advertising billboards to
break out over the countryside. Country clubs, golf courses,
and road houses multiplied to serve the more prosperous;
farmers found it easier to get to villages or to visit one
another, and many began to market their produce through
roadside stands. Hoardes emigrated on wheels to Florida
or California, while wilderness regions were invaded by
millions of sportsmen with rod and gun.[19]

By 1929 the industry gave employment, directly or indirectly, to
nearly four million persons, approximately 8% of the persons engaged in the private economy.[20]

Consumer Durables. The three industries thus far discussed

all manifest in one manner or another the introduction of new

products. In electric utilities and chemicals these products

were often inputs in the production process, although electricity,

of course, was widely adopted to home use and chemicals produced

such consumer nondurables as rayon, bakelite, and cosmetics. The

automobile is classified, on the other hand, as a consumer durable.

It was the first major new product designed specifically for final

consumption. (Here too, though, the automobile industry did play

a part in the production process of other industries by providing

---

[19]Soule, op. cit., p.168

[20]Hession and Sardy, op. cit., p. 619 quote an estimate of
employment of 3,700,000. The percentage is derived by employing
Kendrick's estimate of persons engaged in the private economy in
1929, op. cit., Table A-VII, p. 308, which was 44,836,000.

trucks, buses, and tractors.) Automobiles led the revolution in consumer durables which flowered in the 1920's. The production of consumer durables led the growth in manufacturing with a 300 per cent increase from 1899 to 1929.[21] Included were not only automobiles, but such products as radios, mechanical refrigerators, telephones, toasters, flatirons, etc.. The impact of these new consumer products on the economy should not be underestimated. Consider, for example, radio. Before the autumn of 1920 there was no such thing as radio broadcasting. By 1922, however, sales of radio sets, parts, and accessories amounted to 60 million dollars! Table IV traces the growth of the radio industry through the years prior to 1929. In just eight short years, sales in this one industry increased 1,400 per cent! And radio is but a single example. Never before had consumers been presented with such a wide and exciting variety of new products competing for the consumption dollar.

TABLE IV

SALES OF RADIO SETS, PARTS, AND ACCESSORIES, 1922-1929.

Year	Sales	% Increase
1922	$60,000,000	---
1923	136,000,000	127 %
1924	358,000,000	163
1925	430,000,000	20
1926	506,000,000	18
1927	425,600,000	-16
1928	650,550,000	53
1929	842,548,000	30

Adapted from F.L.Allen, Only Yesterday (New York: Harper & Row, 1964), p. 137.

The Construction Industry. Before leaving the discussion of actual production changes, mention must be made of the growth in construction following World War I. Although the construction industry itself showed few actual gains in productivity--output per man-hour increased only 10% between 1919 and 1929 compared to an increase of 27% for the private domestic economy or 7½% in manufacturing[22]--nonetheless, as a stimulant of economic activity it must be ranked higher than even automobiles.

> That part of the national income arising directly from construction was $2.1 billion in 1919 and rose to $4.2 billion in 1926, thereafter declining slowly, the 1928 figure being $4.0 billion. These totals were larger than those of any single group of manufacturing industries except metals and, for the first three years of the period, textiles and leather.[23]

This period saw the construction of the sky-scraper, the emergence of suburbia, and the criss-crossing of the land with new and improved road networks. Undoubtedly, the stimulus of construction aided the sale of automobiles which in turn required and encouraged the further expansion of construction activity.

Not all industries, of course, joined in this exuberant expansion. Agriculture after the close of the war never did regain its war-time prosperity; other industries to suffer included coal-mining, railroads, shipbuilding, and shoe and leather manufacturing. These, however, were in the minority and their distress was drowned

---

[21]Kendrick, op. cit., Table D-III, p. 467.

[22]Ibid., pp. 465-475.   [23]Soule, op. cit., p. 170.

out by the good fortune of others.

Institutional Changes

The conversion of the United States to a mass consumption society required more than simply the attainment of industrial maturity. In addition to the purely technological adjustments in the structure of production, many institutional pre-conditions had to be satisfied. The specific institutional changes required have been enumerated by Hession and Sardy:

> Among these institutional prerequisites for a consumer society were such developments as the organization of business on a national scale with plants sufficiently large to achieve the economies of mass production; the development of the management skills necessary to conduct such large-scale businesses; the determination of consumer wants and the channeling of the increased discretionary income into demand for goods and services that business was ready to produce--the tasks of market research and advertising. In addition, there was the need to adapt tax policies and private financial practices to the objectives of providing mass purchasing power and credit so that the flood of consumer goods could be bought. Our banking system, which had become increasingly unstable and unreliable, had to be reorganized to permit a greater degree of public control over the business cycle and thus achieve more stable economic growth; this was the task confronting the founders of the Federal Reserve System. Finally, government policies, which in the late nineteenth century had reflected the acceptance of a laissez faire philosophy, had to be adapted to the service and protection of the consumer and the public interest generally.[24]

In the following sections, a brief look will be taken at the manner in which the United States accomplished these institutional changes.

The Merger Movement. One of the first requirements of mass production is size. This condition was readily filled by what has

---

[24] op. cit., p. 539.

been referred to as the first merger movement in the U.S., which occurred before 1903. Spurred on by New Jersey's legislation of the holding company in 1889, the mergers of this period set the stage for the subsequent market structures of American industry.[25]

Although the causes of this merger movement are still being debated,[26] certainly one of the principal reasons was the possibility of economies of scale. The companies which emerged during this period took on a national character: American Sugar Refining, National Casket Company, Continental Can, Federal Steel Company, and United States Steel Corporation; such concerns as these took the entire nation as their market, a necessary precondition to mass production. This first merger movement was followed by a second in the years 1919-30, which, although less spectacular, was actually larger in size than the earlier movement. "Between 1919-30, nearly 12,000 public utility, banking, manufacturing, and mining concerns disappeared; 2,100 mergers occurred, on one count, or about five times the number in the earlier wave."[27]

---

[25] J.S.Bain, Industrial Organization (Homewood, Ill.: Richard D. Irwin, 1959), p. 192.

[26] For a discussion of some of these earlier movements and their causes see R.L.Nelson, Merger Movements in American Industry, 1895-1956 (Princeton: Princeton University Press, 1959); K.E.Boulding The Organizational Revolution (New York:Harper and Bros., 1953); and E.Jones, The Trust Movement in the United States (New York: Macmillan Co., 1921).

[27] Hession and Sardy, op. cit., p. 636.

Although the actual level of concentration in manufacturing
on the average was little affected by these mergers[28] with output
often growing faster than firms could merge, there was a definite
decline in the degree of price competition.[29] This did not mean,
however, that competition as such was curbed. On the contrary,
the period saw an astounding increase in areas of non-price
competition such as service, advertising, and--most significantly
for technological change--product innovation.

Scientific Management. The merger movement provided not
only a change in concentration among sellers, but also an expansion
in the administrative structure of industry. The growth in corporate
size meant that managers had to somehow cope with the immense
increases in size and learn to delegate responsibility. The development of industry throughout the period, thus, resulted not only in
economies of scale in production but also in administration as
managers learned the benefits of specialization of labor. Firms
were now led by groups of specialists: market analysts, lawyers,
bankers, production engineers all combined to replace the solitary
captains of industry of an earlier age. Of great aid to the adminis-
trators of industry was the development during this period of the
idea of scientific management. Developed primarily by Frederick W.
Taylor, scientific management contributed greatly to American
efficiency and the development of the assembly line and mass pro-

---

[28]Bain, op. cit., pp. 203-6.

[29]A.R.Burns,The Decline of Competition(New York: McGraw-
Hill Book Co., 1936)

duction. It stressed such ideas as standardization of products
and processes, improvements of organization, planning and control
of men, machines, and materials, time and motion studies, employee
incentive compensation, and the careful selection   and training
of workers to fit the right man to the right job. Although it is
difficult to quantify the exact impact of these improvements in
the organization and management of industry, it is undeniable that
they played a major role in aiding the advancing productivity of
the period.

Advertising. Mass production requires mass consumption.
It is therefore no surprise that the growth of industry and
increased productivity of the period was accompanied by the
tremenduous increase in advertising expenditures.[30] These, in
turn, provided a direct stimulus to the printing, newspaper and
periodical publishing and paper industries. The total outlay for
advertising in the mid-1920's has been estimated at over one and a
quarter million dollars spread over many outlets:

> Newspapers, $600,000,000; direct advertising (mail
> matters, hand bills, etc.) $300,000,000; magazines,
> $150,000,000; trade papers, $70,000,000; farm papers,
> $27,000,000; sign boards, $30,000,000; novelties,
> $30,000,000; demonstrations, $24,000,000; window displays,
> $20,000,000; posters, $12,000,000; street car cards,
> $11,000,000; motion pictures $5,000,000; programs,
> $5,000,000; total, $1,284,000,000.[31]

---

[30]Factors which account for this growth in advertising
are cited in N.H.Border, The Economic Effects of Advertising (Chicago:
Irwin, 1944), pp. 49-50.

[31]The figures are those of Edward Bok as quoted in Stuart

More than half of the country's output of printed matter was advertising; the ratio of advertising space to total space in newspapers ranged between 40 and 75 per cent; 80 per cent of all mail matter consisted of advertising.[32] The importance of the consuming public had been realized.

Not only was there a massive advertising assault on the public, but the very nature of advertising was transformed from earlier years.

> No longer was it considered enough to recommend one's goods in modest and explicit terms and to place them on the counter in the hope that the ultimate consumer would make up his mind to purchase. The advertiser must plan elaborate national campaigns, consult with psychologists, and employ all the eloquence of poets to cajole, exhort, or intimidate the consumer into buying,--to "break down consumer resistance."[33]

The job of breaking down the consumer's resistance fell not only to the ad-man, but also to the salesman. Never before had such pressure been exerted on salesmen to get results. Firms tried all kinds of gimmicks and contests to stimulate the sales force. A single example, provided by F.L.Allen, should be sufficient to indicate the extent to which pressure was applied: one company

> gave a banquet at which the man with the best score was served with oysters, roast turkey, and a most elaborate

---

Chase, "The Tragedy of Waste," The New Republic, August 19, 1925, reprinted in G.E.Mowry, (ed.), The Twenties, Fords, Flappers & Fanatics (Englewood Cliffs, N.J.: Prentice-Hall, Inc., 1963),p. 15

[32] Ibid., p. 16.

[33] Allen, op. cit., (1964), p. 140.

ice; the man with the second best score had the same
dinner but without the oysters; and so on down to the man
with the worst score, before whom was laid a small plate
of boiled beans and a couple of crackers.[34]

Installment Credit. If the salesman was under pressure,
it is not surprising that consumers undoubtedly felt this pressure
also. But even they could have remained largely successful in
resisting it if not for the introduction of another large scale
innovation of the period: installment credit. Handled largely
by finance companies, installment credit was often extended not
only for automobiles but also for furniture, radios, and various
electric appliances for the home. By the later part of the decade
it has been estimated that 15 % of all retail sales were on an
installment basis and that some six billions of "easy payment"
paper was outstanding.[35] The effect was to keep the factories
roaring although in the process the future was being mortgaged.

Monetary Movements. Although the present survey centers
around technological changes, mention should be made of monetary
movements during the period. The Federal Reserve System had been
inaugurated in 1913 and it was hoped that this would promote the
development of financial stability within the economy. The years
1922 to 1929 have been called the "high tide of the Federal Reserve
System." The very minor recessions which occurred in 1924 and

---

[34] Ibid., p. 141.

[35] Ibid., p. 140.

1927 were to some extent offset by Federal Reserve policies.
However, the challenge posed by the stock market speculation
of 1928 and 1929 and the subsequent Great Crash proved beyond the
capabilities of the Federal Reserve.[36] It is often thought that
the great deflation in the 1930's must have been preceded by a
great inflation in the 1920's. The studies of Friedman and
Schwartz, however, reject this contention. The stock of money
throughout the 1920's remained relatively constant and the stock
market crash resulted in the following years in a quite severe
contraction in the total money supply.[37]

Federal Policies. Before closing the present chapter, a
brief look should be directed at federal policies during the
period. Before the war the Progressive Era sought wide political,
social and economic reforms. After World War I, however, the
reform movement ebbed and government became largely a tool of
business. What was good for business was good for the country.

---

[36]For a discussion and criticisms of FED policies during
these years see M.Friedman and A.J.Schwartz, A Monetary History of
the United States, 1867-1960 (Princeton: Princeton University Press,
1963); E.D.Kemmerer and D.L.Kemmerer, The ABC of the Federal Reserve
System (New York: Harper and Bros., 1950); H.Barger, The Management
of Money (Chicago: Rand, McNally and Co., 1964); L.Currie, "The
Failure of Monetary Policy to Prevent the Depression of 1929-32,"
Journal of Political Economy,XLII (April,1934); A.C.Miller,
"Responsibility for Federal Reserve Policies: 1927-29," American
Economic Review, XXV (September, 1935); and Studenski and Krooss
Financial History of the U.S. (New York: McGraw-Hill Co., 1952).

[37]Friedman and Schwartz, op. cit., (1963), p. 351.

Under the prodding of Andrew W. Mellon, Harding's Secretary of the
Treasury, Congress finally passed the Revenue Act of 1926. In it
the minimum surtax was reduced to 20 per cent; the normal rate of
personal income tax was cut $1\frac{1}{2}$ per cent to 5 per cent; exemptions
under this tax were raised to $1,500 for single persons and $3,500
for married couples; the gift tax was repealed and the maximum
rate on the estate tax was reduced to 20 per cent; and finally,
the capital-stock tax was abolished while the corporate income
tax was increased from $12\frac{1}{2}$ to $13\frac{1}{2}$ per cent.[38] The benevolence of
government to business was evident in other areas,

> ...the Attorneys General under Harding, Coolidge, and
> Hoover were relatively lethargic in their enforcement of
> the antitrust laws; the Supreme Court, dominated by a
> conservative majority; was disposed to maintain the status
> quo, if not turn back the clock. The Federal Trade
> Commission, staffed by appointees who were on the whole
> friendly to business, sought to encourage the 'self-
> regulation' of industry, which had become the new gospel
> of progressive businessmen.[39]

The net effect of government during the period was undeniably
one of encouragement to business expansion.

The present chapter has provided a brief sketch of the major
technological breakthroughs and institutional changes which occurred
in the period prior to and during the acceleration in technological
progress. In the final chapter, these changes will be interpreted
in the light of the aggregate variables of the model developed earlier and will be examined to determine what effect the combined
technological movements might have produced within the economy.

_____

[38]Hession and Sardy, op. cit., p. 682.   [39]Ibid., p. 684.

Chapter VIII

TECHNOLOGY AND THE DISEQUILIBRIUM OF THE 1920'S

The survey of technological changes in the three decades
prior to the great depression, although it may be suggestive,
does not isolate any one particular innovation as responsible for
the acceleration of technology. Indeed, it is questionable
whether any one change could be capable of doubling the rate of
technological progress in the entire economy. What is more likely
is that the simultaneous occurrence of the various innovations of
this transitionary period is the primary cause of the acceleration
in technology. To analyze the impact, then, of the acceleration,
the forces which characterized the growth of this period should
be incorporated into the body of the model. But for the aggregative nature of the analysis, this would be a hopeless task. For-
tunately, all that must be done is to delineate the major kinds of
technological change and the likely impact on the long-run investment function, the short-run investment function, and capacity
output in the economy.

The technological innovations of the period can be grouped
under three broad classifications: (1) those which resulted in new
or improved capital equipment; (2) organizational innovations which
increased the productivity of existing capital; and finally, (3)
the widespread introduction of new consumer products. These
three types of technological change will be examined to determine
their likely effects on the long-run investment function. Before

201

doing this, however, factor price movements during these years should be examined since they also influenced investment spending.

Factor Price Movements

Table V below provides information on the movement of wages, interest rates, and the price of capital goods in the decade after the war. Total hourly compensation in manufacturing increased 13% over the decade. Column (2) provides an index of the movements in the yield of 30-year corporate bonds which decreased some 7 per cent. The cost of capital equipment is given by the index of column (3) which indicates a decrease of slightly over 5 per cent. To arrive at an approximate estimate of the operating cost of capital, the long-term interest rate is multiplied by the cost of capital. The resulting index is given in column (4) showing a decline of 12 per cent. Dividing column (1) by column (4) gives the relative factor price ratio. The cost of labor relative to that of capital during this period showed an increase of nearly 30 per cent. The measures employed here are quite crude and great faith should not be placed in any of the precise percentage estimates. The direction of movement, however, does correspond with results cited by Soule. He indicated an increase in manufacturing wages during this decade of some 17 per cent and a corresponding decrease in the price of capital equipment of about 3 per cent. His results also indicate an increase in wages relative to capital cost.[1] This relative increase in labor costs would rotate the long-

---

[1] G. Soule, Prosperity Decade: From War to Depression, 1917-1929 (New York: Harper & Row, 1968).

TABLE V

FACTOR PRICE MOVEMENTS, 1919-1929.
(1929-100)

Year	Wages[a] (1)	Interest[b] (2)	Price of Capital[c] (3)	Capital Cost (4)	Factor Price Ratio (5)
1919	88.5	107.5	105.6	113.5	78.0
1920	88.7	115.4	119.8	138.2	64.2
1921	87.7	117.0	102.5	119.9	73.1
1922	86.6	106.6	92.0	98.1	88.3
1923	94.1	104.3	99.1	103.4	91.0
1924	97.0	105.4	98.7	104.0	93.3
1925	93.9	101.8	97.6	99.4	94.5
1926	93.9	99.5	97.3	96.0	97.8
1927	96.7	97.3	96.7	94.1	102.8
1928	97.8	91.6	97.0	88.9	101.0
1929	100.0	100.0	100.0	100.0	100.0

Above data obtained from Long-Term Economic Growth,
U.S. Department of Commerce, Bureau of the Census, 1966.

[a]Table B72, pp. 202-3, total compensation per hour at
work manufacturing production workers, 1957 dollars.

[b]Table B82, pp. 204-5, basic yields of 1-year corporate
bonds.

[c]Table B67, pp. 200-1, implicit price deflator for
fixed investment.

run investment   function upward, providing a stimulus to the economy.

The Impact of Technological Change

The net change in long-run investment cannot   be determined
until the effects of changing efficiency are considered. Depending
on the type of technological change, the influence on LRI may
be in conflicting directions. Of the three major movements in
technology mentioned earlier, the first was the development of
technical improvements embodied only in new capital equipment.
The development of electric power certainly falls in this category.
Increases in power available through the electrification of industry could not be obtained unless electrical equipment were actually
purchased and installed and many of the machines benefiting from
electrical power would, of course, have to be purchased. The
development of the chemical industry and the new products created
there were often used in the production process. There they served
to increase considerably the productivity of industry. However,
the materials had to be purchased before any benefits were derived.
Assembly line techniques used in automobile production also fall
in this category. Although occasionally, production could be
placed on an assembly line without any installation of new equipment, generally this was not the case. Once again, the innovation
was embodied in new equipment which first had to be purchased
through investment expenditures before any benefits were realized.

This particular form of technological change has the immediate effect of shifting the long-term investment function upward,
thus reinforcing the effect of factor-price changes. The avail-

ability of these new innovations made current capital equipment in many industries obsolete. This acceleration in the rate
of depreciation is reflected in the rotation of the long-run
investment function. Investment levels would remain relatively
high until the new innovations had been incorporated into the
existing capital stock through purchase and replacement of obsolescent capital.

The second major form of technological innovation improved
the productivity of the entire stock of capital. Such innovations
as scientific management, the merger movement, and increases in
administrative efficiency come under this heading. Another improvement which could be cited in this regard is the increased
efficiency in the method of distribution of final products.
With the availability of automobiles and trucks, markets were expanded and firms could sell their products in markets not previously available. In addition, the chain stores, which developed
during the 1920's, realized great savings in cost without actually
increasing the physical capital stock. The net effect of innovations such as these would be to improve the efficiency of the
existing stock of capital. The LRI function would be rotated
downward, the opposite direction of the earlier forces. Unlike
the earlier forces, however, this technological innovation would
represent a permanent downward rotation. The upward shift due to
technological innovations results in increased investment spending
only so long as current technology makes existing equipment obsolete. Once the new equipment is purchased and installed, this

influence disappears and the long-run investment function shifts
downward not merely to its original position, but beyond since
the installation of the new capital equipment indicates that the
capital stock is now capapble of producing an output greater than
it had been earlier. Thus, though the downward shift of the
investment function might be delayed for a time, eventually the
rate of investment spending would decline.

The third major innovation of these years is found in the
consumer rather than the capital goods industries. And this is
simply the tremenduous onrush of new consumer products. The
automobile, the radio, rayon, cosmetics, the entire field of
electrical home appliances, all are found in this category. Although the effect on productivity is not as clear-cut here, these
products represent major advances in technology nonetheless. The
fact that these new products were developed at all indicates that
the rate of return expected from the employment of the economy's
resources in developing these goods exceeded that available in
the production of current products. Resources available for
production are limited. If profits, or potential profits, available
through the development of a new product are greater than those
being obtained in the production of existing lines, then resources
should be switched to the new products. The return on investment
will be greater and, hence, so will productivity in the economy.

The effect of this type of innovation on the LRI function
is felt in two respects. Initially, long-run investment is shifted
upward because of the possibility of profitable exploitation of

the new products. The influence, however, is greater than this
single force would imply. Since the products are new, there are
no current stocks of the product. As a result, in the growth
stage of these industries output rates would be extraordinarily
high due to high levels of demand. When the automobile ceased
being a luxury of the rich and evolved into a necessity of the
many, automobile production could continue at extremely high
rates as the great backlog of demand was gradually filled. The
same was true of radio. By the beginning of the decade radio
did not exist; by the end of the decade the radio was a common
feature of the home. The development of rayon allowed millions
of women in the country to attain a luxury they could never before
have afforded: silk stockings. All of the new consumer durables
and nondurables fall into this class. Their introduction and
acceptance meant an initial period of very high sales as the
great backlog in demand was being filled. But these backlogs
would eventually be filled. The demand for these products would
gradually slow down, if not diminish altogether production rates
would have to diminish to replacement levels. Investment, geared
as it is to expected versus actual capacity operation, would decline.
The result, then, of the development of these new products would
be an upward shift in the long-run investment function. This shift
could be attributed largely to what could be called autonomous
forces as the young industries sought to fill the great gaps in
demand. However, when these gaps were filled, this element in
investment would inevitably decline.

The analysis of technological change during the period
indicates that the probable changes in long-run, and hence short-
run, investment could be represented by an upward rotation of the
long-run investment function early in the period and high levels
of autonomous investment spending throughout much of the period.
The installation of new, more efficient capital, and the development of improved production techniques, would, however, eventually
become dominant, pushing the LRI function downward. From the
earlier analysis of Chapter V, the result should have been a
slowing down in the economy if not an outright recession. Except
for two very minor interruptions in 1924 and 1927, this did not,
in fact, occur during the 1920's. Both investment levels and
aggregate expenditure remained high beyond the date that might
have been expected to call forth internal adjustments in the system.
When the crash did come, instead of the normal recession called
for in the course of adjustment, the economy experienced one of
the greatest depressions in its history with respect to both
length and severity. How was it that the economy became so unbalanced and that this maladjustment continued for so long? To
find the answer to these questions, attention must be shifted to
the demand side of the picture through these years.

Movements in Aggregate Demand

Demand pressure was high because of industries experiencing
innovational advances. But it was extraordinarily high for other
reasons as well. As mentioned in Chapter VII, construction experienced a considerable boom during these years and other sectors of

the economy were experiencing high levels of investment, not
necessarily because of any technological changes on their part,
but because of the high levels of over-all aggregate demand.
The most important maladjustment, however, probably emanated from
the consuming sector of the economy.

Two major institutional changes of the period can be pointed
to as significantly shifting the relationship between consumption
and real income: advertising and installment credit. The combined
pressure of the advertiser and the salesman harking their previously unavailable products undoubtedly had a major impact on
consumer spending. The result would be an upward shift in the
consumption function, or what is the same thing, a downward shift
in savings. This downward shift in savings was augmented by the
introduction of consumer installment credit. Consumers were able
to maintain total consumption demand on the basis of income not
yet earned. Although the effects of advertising and high-pressure
salesmanship could be expected to produce more or less a permanent
alternation in the consumption function, installment credit could
not unless incomes continued to rise with production. The fact
that they did not meant that eventually, there would be a drop in
consumer demand, in fact, a major drop as current incomes could
not be used to buy current products but rather had to be allocated
to products purchased earlier.

It might be useful to stop and examine for a moment the
position of consumer finances during these years. The period was
one of considerable prosperity with wages, both monetary and real,

increasing during the twenties. However, the actual increase
in labor income fell far short of the gains in productivity.
The major benefits of the increased technology fell to profits.
This only served to magnify an already unbalanced distribution of
income. Leuchtenburg has estimated that 71 per cent of all
American families had incomes of under $2,500 in 1929; a figure
then considered the minimum level for a decent standard of living.
The period saw concurrently increases in the number of extremely
wealthy and extremely poor families. The 36,000 richest families
in the nation received the same total income as the 12,000,000
poorest--42% of American families received under $1,500 a year.[2]
Industry had discovered the benefits of mass consumption, but
seemed reluctant to follow that discovery to its logical conclusion.
Industry could not continue to sell an increasingly large number
of products to a large segment of the population and keep most
of the earned income in the form of profits rather than passing
it back to the population in the form of wages. Under these
conditions, the shift in the consumption function during the 1920's
could only be temporary. Sooner or later, the consumer segment
of aggregate demand would have to fall back to its normal position;
in fact, farther than its normal position.

At the same time, as the decade drew to a close, the
other segments of aggregate demand were also beginning to show

---

[2] W.E.Leuchtenberg, The Perils of Prosperity, 1919-1932.
(Chicago: University of Chicago Press, 1958),pp.193-4.

signs of slowing down. Construction had managed to catch up
with housing demand. By 1929 residential construction expenditure
had fallen to three billion dollars. In 1925 it had been five
billion. Automobiles continued their growth, but the backlog
in demand here, too, was gradually becoming satisfied. The
result was a cutback in orders for the industries supplying
the automobile industry: steel, rubber, glas, etc., as the rate
of the rate of growth of automobile production began to slow down.
The bulk of the increased investment potentialities due to
technological change had been realized and capacity was catching
up with demand. The inevitable result was a slowing down in
investment expenditures. In fact, Maclaurin has noted a change
in the innovative character of the automobile industry by the
late 1920's. He cites several reasons for this change:
"the quality of entrepreneurial leadership, the absence of a
research conception, the explosive rate of previous growth,
and the success of the established oligopoly."[3] In terms of the
explanation offered here, the reason for this apparent change is
that the innovational possibilities had been exploited and, in
the process, the capacity of the automobile industry to produce
cars had caught up with the expected rate of sale of cars. Under
these conditions, new technological improvements would not be
undertaken to expand already sufficient capacity.

---

[3] W.R. Maclaurin, "Innovation and Capital Formation in Some
American Industries," Capital Formation and Economic Growth,
Universities-National Bureau Committee for Economic Research
(Princeton: Princeton University Press, 1955). p. 554.

The Disequilibrium of the 1920's

The situation as it might have appeared in the later half of the 1920's is depicted in Fig. 40. Technological possibilities during and before the decade had resulted in an upward shift of the long-run investment function to LRI_2. The installation of the new productive equipment and the other technological innovations increasing the productivity of fixed capital would have rotated the investment function downward back towards the long-run savings curve. In the normal course of events, the boom in investment would have been curbed as capacity neared actual operation and long-run investment approached long-run savings. However, the 1920's were not the normal course of events. For the various reasons cited above, it is probable that the long-run savings function was altered during these years. Thus as the LRI curve moved downward, it remained above savings for an extended period because the savings function itself was moving downward. Assume the shift in LRS reached the position LRS_2 and stabilized there sometime in the mid to later 20's. The continual installation of new equipment and adoption of improved distributional and organizational arrangements would cause the LRI to continue its downward movement. For much of the time, however, investment would exceed savings and the economy would be operating at high capacity levels. Eventually, however, the capital stock and increased optimal capacity would catch up with current or anticipated output rates; desired investment would fall below desired savings. The result would be a slowing of aggregate demand and a reduction of output.

Whether or not the reduction resulted in a minor recession or a deep depression depended mainly on the speed of the reduction in demand. A gradual reduction could be caught by the central equilibrium position and growth could continue from that point. A major reduction, however, would shift the economy down toward the depressionary equilibrium. Needless to say, the events of the period all contributed toward making the crash, when it did finally come, a major reduction.

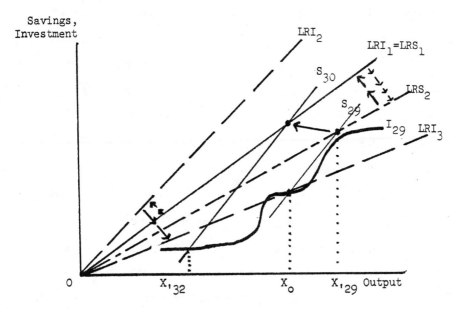

Fig. 40.--The shifting LRI and LRS functions leading to the Great Depression.

Leuchtenberg[4] has stated that it was primarily the stock market boom of the later 1920's which postponed the inevitable

---

[4] <u>op</u>. <u>cit</u>., p. 246.

collapse brought about by the decreasing investment opportunities and subsequent decline in investment expenditures. Profits, which were mentioned earlier in connection with the maldistribution of income, played an important role here. The productivity advances made during these years resulted in high income levels which went primarily into profits rather than wages. As investment opportunities in real capital diminished, what happened to these funds? To be sure, dividends increased over the period some 65%, but the bulk of the increase in profits, 62% between 1923 and 1929, most likely found its way into stock market speculation. There was a mass movement on the part of industry to invest surplus funds in speculation which, at the time, appeared more profitable than investing in actual capital expansion. The volume of sales on the New York Stock Exchange increased 277% between 1923 and 1928. As a result of this massive stock market speculation, a good portion of the income earned in production was being channeled back not as a demand for more real goods, but as a demand for financial assets.

In the last year or two before the crash, the disequilibrium of the economy was becoming more and more precarious. Consumption was being maintained by installment buying and, in fact, encouraged by the paper profits many thought they were earning in stocks, increases in wealth which proved later to be illusory. Investment expenditures had already been decreasing as capacity neared demand. The prosperity would only be continued if consumers could increase consumption to match the declining investment. The possibility of this occurring was shattered by the crash of 1929.

It is undeniable that the market crash played a major role
in precipitating the Great Depression. It destroyed simultaneously
both business and consumer confidence. Yet the economy had before
encountered stock market collapses. What made the crash of 1929
so catastrophic? From the consumer side of the market, the crash
not only initiated the usual reduction in aggregate demand, but
most likely was the stimulus which caused the long-run savings
function to shift back toward its normal position (LRS_2 moves
back to LRS_1 in Fig. 40.) Purchases on installment credit were
sharply curtailed. The money supply in the economy suffered a
serious contraction as bank after bank was forced to close. In
1929 over 600 banks failed; the following year the number jumped
to over 1,300; in 1931 another 2,300 were forced to close their
doors. The effect of these bank closures on consumer confidence
and spending cannot be exaggerated. The failure of the Bank of
the United States in New York City with 400,000 depositors affected
approximately one third of the entire population of the city.[5]
The life-savings of many were wiped out. This colossal collapse
of wealth throughout the economy would result in a striking shift
in the consumption function.

With the long-run savings function being shifted rapidly
back upward and with long-run investment stationary in its new
lower level, no equilibrium except the depressionary one would be

_____

[5]Ibid., p. 256.

conceivable. In Fig. 40, the economy would move from $X_{,29}$ downward
toward $X_{,32}$. Here lay the reasons why the depression was as severe
as it was and why it lasted so long. The improvement in technology
resulted in a substantial increase in the economy's capacity to
produce. In the normal course of events, improving technology
will result eventually in a slowing down of investment and a
subsequent readjustment in the economy to the new conditions. This
slowing down, however, was delayed in the 1920's. The continual
improvement in the capacity to produce was allowed to continue
far beyond requirements because of the simultaneous high levels
of autonomous investment and the probable shift in consumer
demand during this period. These two forces served to mask the
rise in capacity relative to long-run demand. When the collapse
finally did come, the savings function was shifted rudely back
toward its normal position and the subsequent decline in demand
brought net investment to negative levels. The way out of the
depression would come only when aggregate demand increased
sufficiently that current capacity became, once again, insufficient,
or when the capital stock depreciated, decreasing optimal capacity
toward actual output rates. The great increase in productivity
and capacity during the period would inevitably have taken many,
many years to disappear; the depression was understandably a
long one.

Chapter IX

SUMMARY

This study has developed a macro-economic model capable
of analyzing the effects of short-run movements in such parameters as factor prices and technical change. The primary goal
has been an investigation of the likely impact of the accelerating
technical progress of the 1920's and the connection, if any,
between this acceleration in technology and the subsequent Great
Depression.

The introductory chapter lays out the framework of the
problem and discusses the various empirical studies confirming
the assumed acceleration in technical change. Four separate
methods of estimating the rate of technical change all arrive
at the same conclusion. Whether the rate of technical change is
estimated through productivity ratios employing an arithmetic
index (Kendrick, Schmookler), or a geometric index (Solow), or
the parameters of a linear regression analysis (Brown), or by the
implications of economic growth theory (Vanek), the result is
the same. The rate of technical progress accelerated from
approximately 1% per year prior to 1920 to approximately 2% per
year after 1920. Assuming, then, this acceleration in technology,
the question next asked is what would be the likely short-run
effects on the aggregate economy?

Chapters II, III, and IV build up the foundation of a
macroeconomic model capable of answering the above question. In

217

Chapter II the aggregate supply curve is derived and the relationship between the current rate of output and the desired capital
stock specified. The desired capital stock is seen to be a
function of the current rate of output, the current factor prices,
and the current state of technology. To combine the aggregate
supply curve with an aggregate demand curve, Chapter III provides
a discussion of the concepts underlying the aggregate demand curve,
and demonstrates how the rate of real output and the price level
could be determined.

Crucial to any study of short-run economic movements is
the investment function. Chapter IV provides a long discussion
of the determinants of aggregate investment. Assuming that firms
attempt to maximize profits through investment, investment in any given period will be determined by the difference
between the increase in profits expected from that investment
and the increase in costs likely to accompany the investment. A
limit on the rate of investment for any given period exists
because of the rapidly accelerating costs of capital expansion
encountered when the rate of investment exceeds the existing
rate of savings and the capacity of the capital goods industry
is strained. A lower limit of zero gross investment also, obviously,
exists. This particular form of the investment function is similar
to that developed by Kaldor and by Vanek. The similarities and
dissimilarities are pointed out in Chapter IV. By adjusting the
shape of the premium cost function, however, another form of the
aggregate investment function appears. If it is assumed that

any net investment is subject to a discontinuous increase in costs (or that there is a rapid rise in investment costs between internal and external financing), the marginal propensity to invest in the neighborhood of the optimal rate of output will be quite low. In other words, if the actual rate of output is quite near the optimal rate of output, then the firms' estimate of the desired stock of capital will be little affected and, hence, so too will investment expenditures. With the investment function assuming this particular form, three stable equilibrium positions are possible. In addition to the deflationary and inflationary equilibriums, there will be also a stable central equilibrium near the optimal rate of output.

Chapter V explores the implications of changing parametric values. To aid in the analysis of movements over time, the concepts of long-run savings and long-run investment are introduced. It is found that over a long-run period the average propensity to invest must remain approximately equal to the average propensity to save. However, over short-run periods, the divergence of long-run investment from long-run savings is likely to lead to a disequilibrium producing fluctuations in the rate of real output.

Although steady state growth is possible in the model, given the appropriate movements in the parameters of the system, cyclical movements are also quite possible. Chapter VI thus reviewes the major theories of business cycle movements and demonstrates how the present model was consistent with all of these theories provided only that the appropriate parametric assumptions are made. To

analyze the events occurring during the 1920's it is necessary to
specify how the parameters of the system behaved. Thus, Chapter VII
explores the movements of the general economy in the period from
1899 to 1929. Particular emphasis is placed on the events which
most likely played a part in the acceleration in the rate of
technical progress. Of major importance in this respect were the
development of the electric power industry, the growth of automobiles
and chemicals, in addition to the flood of new consumer products. These
are all examples of the case in point. Institutional changes
also played a role, note the development of the Federal Reserve
System, consumer installment credit, and advertising.

In Chapter VIII, the model developed is used to analyze
the events leading up to the Great Depression. The conclusion
reached here is that the accelerating technical change would
lead to an increase in investment expenditures attempting to
incorporate the change, followed by a subsequent decline, that
is, the normal business cycle. However, a number of other factors
occurring simultaneously with the acceleration in technology,
altered the normal course of events. It is probable that the
consumption function underwent a shift during the 1920's due to
the availability of new products and the credit with which to buy
them, in addition to the high-pressure salesmanship and advertising
prevalent during the period. Autonomous investment expenditures,
due largely to the construction boom, were also extraordinarily
high during these years. As a result of the above forces, the

excessive capacity being built up was masked by the high levels
of consumption and investment spending.

The stock-market crash in 1929, destroying as it did
much of the paper wealth in the economy, was undoubtedly a stimulus
shifting consumption spending back toward and beyond normal levels.
The drop in aggregate demand led to a corresponding decrease in
investment expenditures which only magnified the decreasing
rates of real output. The rapid shift in consumption in the face
of the new productive capacity in the economy, illustrated by a
long-run investment function considerably below its more "normal"
level, resulted in only one possible outcome: movement toward
the depressionary equilibrium. The existing stock of capital
was far above the new desired capital stock. The economy was
trapped in a depression which would take a long period of time
to escape from as is evidenced by the length of the Great Depression.

In considering the implications for the future, it is unlikely
that the economy should experience a disequilibrium as serious as
that which enveloped the 1930's. The cause of that depression was
buried not only in advancing technology, but also in simultaneous
institutional changes shifting consumer demand. If consumer demand
had remained stationary throughout the period, that is, if the long-
run savings function had not shifted, the effects of the improved
technology would have been incorporated into the economy long before
1929, investment levels would have declined and a recession would
have occurred. It need not, however, have been a major recession
and growth could have been continued in a relatively short time.

BIBLIOGRAPHY

A. ARTICLES

Abramovitz, Moses. "Economic Growth in the United States,"
  American Economic Review, LII (September, 1962), 762-82.

_____, "Resource and Output Trends in the United States
  since 1870," American Economic Review, XLVI (May, 1956), 5-23.

Aftalion, Albert. "The Theory of Economic Cycles Based on the
  Capitalist Technique of Production," Review of Economics
  and Statistics, IX (October, 1927), 165-70.

Alexander, Sidney Stuart. "Issues of Business Cycle Theory
  Raised by Mr. Hicks," American Economic Review, XLI
  (December, 1951), 861-78.

Armano, Akihiro. "Biased Technical Progress and a Neoclassical
  Theory of Economic Growth," Quarterly Journal of Economics,
  LXXVIII (February, 1964), 129-38.

Ando, Albert and George Leland Bach. "The Redistributional Effects
  of Inflation," Review of Economics and Statistics, XXXIX
  (February, 1957), 1-13.

_____, and Franco Modigliani. "The 'Life Cycle' Hypothesis of
  Saving: Aggregate Implications and Tests," American Economic
  Review, LIII (March, 1963), 55-84.

Asimakopulos, A. "The Definition of Neutral Inventions," Economic
  Journal, LXXIII (December, 1963), 675-80.

_____, and John Cathcart Weldon, "The Classification of Technical
  Progress in Models of Economic Growth," Economica, XXX (November,
  1963), 372-86.

Bator, Francis M. "Capital Productivity, Input Allocation and
  Growth," Quarterly Journal of Economics, LXXI (February, 1957),
  86-106.

Belfer, Nathan. "Implications of Capital-Saving Inventions,"
  Social Research, XVI (September, 1949), 353-365.

Blaug, Mark. "A Survey of the Theory of Process Innovations,"
  Economica, XXX (February, 1963), 13-32.

Brown, Howard R., and Gerald M. Meier, "Institutional Aspects of
  Economic Fluctuations," in Post-Keynesian Economics, Kenneth
  Kurihara, editor. New Brunswick, New Jersey: Rutgers University
  Press, 1954. Pp. 155-169.

Bowman, Raymond T., and Almarin Phillips. "The Capacity Concept and Induced Investment," _Canadian Journal of Economics and Political Science_, XXI (May, 1955), 190-203.

Brems, Hans. "Growth Rates of Output, Labor Force Hours and Productivity," _Review of Economics and Statistics_, XXXIX (November, 1957), 415-20.

Broster, Eric James. "An Economic Analysis of Fixed Investment," _Economic Journal_, LXVIII (December, 1958), 768-79.

Brown, Murray. "Profits, Output and Liquidity in the Theory of Fixed Investment," _International Economic Review_, II (January, 1961), 110-121.

_____, and Joel Popkin, "A Measure of Technological Change and Returns to Scale, _Review of Economics and Statistics_, XLIV (November, 1962), 402-11.

Brozen, Yale. "Adapting to Technological Change," _Journal of Business_, XXIV (April, 1951), 114-26.

_____, "Determinants of the Direction of Technological Change," _American Economic Review_, XLIII (May, 1953), 288-302.

Chase, Stuart. "The Tragedy of Waste," _The New Republic_, August 19, 1925.

Chenery, Hollis Burnley. "Overcapacity and the Acceleration Principle," _Econometrica_, XX (January, 1952), 1-28.

Cobb, Charles W., and Paul H. Douglas, "A Theory of Production," _American Economic Review_, XVIII (March, 1928), 139-65.

Currie, Lauchlin. "The Failure of Monetary Policy to Prevent the Depression of 1929-32," _Journal of Political Economy_, XLII (April, 1934), 145-77.

Denison, Edward F. "The Unimportance of the Embodied Question," _American Economic Review_, LIV (March, 1964), 90-94.

Diamond, Peter A. "Technical Change and the Measurement of Capital and Output," _Review of Economic Studies_, XXXII (October, 1965), 289-98.

Domar, Evsey David. "Depreciation, Replacement and Growth," _Economic Journal_, LXVI (December, 1957), 655-8.

_____. "On the Measurement of Technological Change," _Economic Journal_, LXX (December, 1961), 709-29.

Duesenberry, James. "Hicks on the Trade Cycle," _Quarterly Journal of Economics_, LXIV (August, 1950), 464-76.

_____. "Innovation and Growth," _American Economic Review_, XLVI (May, 1956), 134-41.

Eckaus, Richard Samuel. "The Acceleration Principle Reconsidered," _Quarterly Journal of Economics_, LXVII (May, 1953), 209-230.

Eisner, Robert. "Technological Change, Obsolescence and Aggregate Demand," _American Economic Review_, XLVI (March, 1956), 92-105.

_____, and Robert H. Strotz. "Determinants of Business Investment," in _Impacts of Monetary Policy_, Commission on Money and Credit. Englewood Cliffs, New Jersey, 1963). Pp.60-338.

England, Minnie Throop. "Promotion as the Cause of Crises," _Quarterly Journal of Economics_, XXIX (August, 1915), 748-67.

Fellner, William John. "The Capital-Output Ratio in Dynamic Economics," in _Money, Trade and Economic Growth_

Ferber, Robert. "Research on Household Behavior," _American Economic Review_, LII (March, 1962), 19-63.

Fisher, Franklin Marvin. "Embodied Technical Change and the Existence of an Aggregate Capital Stock," _Review of Economic Studies_, XXXII (October, 1965), 263-88.

Fisher, Gene Harvey. "A Survey of the Theory of Induced Investment, 1900-1940," _Southern Economic Journal_, XVIII (April, 1952), 474-94.

Foss, Murray. "The Utilization of Capital Equipment," _Survey of Current Business_, (June, 1963), 8-16.

Frankel, Marvin. "Obsolescence and Technological Change in a Maturing Economy," _American Economic Review_, XLV (June, 1955) 296-319.

Friedman, Milton. "The Demand for Money: Some Theoretical and Empirical Results," _Journal of Political Economy_, LXVII (August, 1959), 327-51.

_____. "The Lag in Effect of Monetary Policy," _Journal of Political Economy_, LXIX (October, 1961), 447-66.

_____. "A Monetary and Fiscal Framework for Economic Stability," _American Economic Review_, XXXVIII (June, 1948), 245-64.

_____. "The Supply of Money and Change in Prices and Output," The Relationship of Prices to Economic Stability and Growth, Compendium, pp. 241-56. United States Congress Joint Economic Committee Document No. 23734, March 31, 1958. Washington, D.C.: Government Printing Office, 1958.

_____, and Anna J. Schwartz, "Money and Business Cycles," The Review of Economics and Statistics, Supplement, XLV (February, 1963), 32-64.

Frisch, Ragnar. "Propagation Problems and Impulse Problems in Dynamic Economics," in Essays in Honor of Gustav Cassel, London: George Allen and Unwin, Ltd., 1933. Reprinted in Readings in Business Cycles, American Economic Association. Homewood, Ill.: Richard D. Irwin, 1965.

Gilbert, John Cannon. "Changes in Productivity and the Price Level in a Closed Economy," Yorkshire Bulletin of Economic and Social Research, VIII (November, 1956), 61-79.

Goodwin, R. M. "A Model of Cyclical Growth" in The Business Cycle in the Post-War World, Erik Lundberg, editor. London: Macmillan & Co., Ltd., 1955. Pp. 203-221.

Goodwin, Richard Murphy. "The Nonlinear Accelerator and the Persistence of Business Cycles," Econometrica, XIX (January, 1951), 1-17.

_____. "Secular and Cyclical Aspects of the Multiplier and the Accelerator," Income, Employment and Public Policy: Essays in Honor of Alvin H. Hansen. New York: W. W. Norton, 1948.

Gordon, Donald Flemming. "Obsolescence and Technological Change: A Comment," (followed by Marvin Frankel's reply.) American Economic Review, XLVI (September, 1956), 646-52.

Gordon, Robert Aaron. "Investment Behavior and Business Cycles," Review of Economics and Statistics, XXXVII (February, 1955), 23-34.

Green, H. A. J. "Embodied Progress, Investment and Growth," American Economic Review, LVI (March, 1966), 138-51.

Gregory, Sir Theodore Emanuel. "Rationalisation and Technological Unemployment," The Economic Journal, XL (December, 1930), 551-67.

Haberler, Gottfried. "Monetary and Real Factors Affecting Economic Stability: A Critique of Certain Tendencies in Modern Economic Theory," Banca Nazionale Del Lavoro Quarterly Review, IX (September, 1956). Reprinted in Readings in Business Cycles, American Economic Association. Homewood, Ill.: Richard D. Irwin, 1965, Pp. 130-49.

Hahn, Frank H.,and R. C. O. Matthews. "The Theory of Economic
Growth: A Survey," Economic Journal, LXXIV (December, 1964),
779-902.

Hamberg, Daniel. "Production Functions, Innovations and Economic
Growth," Journal of Political Economy, LXVII (June, 1959), 238-45.

Harcourt, G. C. "Productivity and Technical Change," Economic
Record, XXXVIII (September, 1962), 388-94.

Harrod, Sir Roy Forbes. "The 'Neutrality' of Improvements,"
Economic Journal, LXXI (June, 1961), 300-304.

Heller, Walter W. "The Anatomy of Investment Decisions," Harvard
Business Review, XXIX (March, 1951), 95-103.

Henderson, Ronald Frank. "Industrial Investment in Fixed Capital:
A Reconsideration," Scottish Journal of Political Economy,
III (October, 1956), 177-87.

Hickman, Bert George. "Capacity, Capacity Utilization and the
Acceleration Principle," Studies in Income and Wealth,
Vol. XIX. National Bureau of Economic Research. Princeton:
Princeton University Press, 1957. Pp. 419-49.

_____. "Diffusion, Acceleration, and Business Cycles," American
Economic Review, XLIX (September, 1959), 535-65.

Hicks, John Richard. "Mr. Keynes and the 'Classics': A Suggested
Interpretation," Econometrica, V (April, 1937), 147-59.

Hirshleifer, Jack. "On the Theory of Optimal Investment Decision,"
Journal of Political Economy, LXVI (August, 1958), 329-52.

Hogan, Warren P. "Technical Progress and Production Functions,"
(followed by Robert Solow's reply), Review of Economics and
Statistics, XL (November, 1958), 407-11.

Howrey, E. Philip. "Technical Change, Capital Longevity, and
Economic Growth," American Economic Review, Supplement, LV
(May, 1965), 397-410.

Ichimura, Shinichi. "Toward a General Nonlinear Macrodynamic Theory
of Economic Fluctuations," in Post-Keynesian Economics,
Kenneth Kurihara, editor.

Johnston, R. E. "Technical Progress and Innovation," Oxford Economic
Papers, XVIII (July, 1966), 158-76.

Jorgenson, Dale W. "Anticipations and Investment Behavior," in
The Brookings Quarterly Econometric Model of the United States,
James Duesenberry, et. al. editors. Chicago: Rand McNally and
Co., 1965. Pp. 35-94.

_____. "The Embodiment Hypothesis," Journal of Political Economy,
LXXIV (February, 1966), 1-17.

_____, and Zvi Griliches. "Capital Theory: Technical Progress
and Capital Structure," American Economic Review, Supplement,
LVI (May, 1966), 50-61.

_____, and Zvi Griliches. "The Explanation of Productivity
Change," Review of Economic Studies, XXXIV (July, 1967),249-83.

_____, and Zvi Griliches. "Sources of Measured Productivity
Change: Capital Input," American Economic Review, LVI

_____, and Robert E. Hall. "Tax Policy and Investment Behavior,"
American Economic Review, LVII (June, 1967), 391-414.

_____, and Calvin D. Siebert, "A Comparison of Alternative
Theories of Corporate Investment Behavior," American Economic
Review, LVIII (September, 1968), 681-712.

Jung, Clarence. "Investment Decisions and the Non-linear Cycle,"
Journal of Industrial Economics, IV (October, 1955), 33-44.

Kaldor, Nicholas. "A Case Against Technical Progress?" Economica,
XII (May, 1932), 180-196.

_____. "A Model of the Trade Cycle," Economic Journal, L
(March, 1940), 78-92.

Kendrick, John W., and Ryuzo Sato. "Factor Prices, Productivity
and Economic Growth," American Economic Review, LIII
(December, 1963), 974-1003.

Kennedy, Charles. "The Character of Improvements and of Technical
Progress," Economic Journal, LXXII (December, 1962), 899-911.

_____. "Technical Progress and Investment," Economic Journal,
LXXI (June, 1961), 292-99.

Kindleberger, Charles Poor. "Obsolescence and Technical Change,"

Klein, Lawrence R. "Studies in Investment Behavior," Conference
on Business Cycles. New York: National Bureau of Economic
Research, 1951. Pp. 233-303.

Knox, A. D. "The Acceleration Principle and the Theory of Investment: A Survey," Economica, XIX (August, 1952), 269-297.

Koyck, Leen M., and Hendrieke Goris. "The Prices of Investment Goods and the Volume of Production in the United States," Review of Economics and Statistics, XXXV (February, 1953),59-66.

Lerner, Abba P. "On some Recent Developments in Capital Theory," American Economic Review, LV (May, 1965), 284-95.

Levine, Herbert S. "A Small Problem in the Analysis of Growth," Review of Economics and Statistics, XLII (May, 1960), 225-8.

Maclaurin, Rupert W. "Innovation and Capital Formation in Some American Industries," Capital Formation and Economic Growth, Universities-National Bureau Committee for Economic Research. Princeton: Princeton University Press, 1955. Pp. 551-572.

_____. "The Process of Technological Innovation: The Launching of a New Scientific Industry," American Economic Review, XL (March, 1950), 90-112.

_____. "The Sequence from Invention to Innovation and its Relation to Economic Growth," Quarterly Journal of Economics, LXVII (February, 1953), 97-111.

Manne, Alan Sussimann. "Some Notes on the Acceleration Principle," Review of Economics and Statistics, XXVII (May, 1945), 93-9.

_____, and John M. Frankovich. "Electronic Calculating Methods for Handling the Excess Capacity Problem," Review of Economics and Statistics, XXXV (February, 1953), 51-8.

Mansfield, Edwin. "Technical Change and the Rate of Imitation," Econometrica, XXIX (October, 1961), 741-66.

Massell, Benton F. "Capital Formation and Technological Change in United States Manufacturing," Review of Economics and Statistics, XLII (May, 1960), 182-88.

_____. "Investment, Innovation and Growth," Econometrica, XXX (April, 1962), 239-52.

Matthews, R. C. O. "Capital Stock Adjustment Theories of the Trade Cycle and the Problem of Policy," in Post-Keynesian Economics, Kenneth Kurihara, editor.

Metzler, Lloyd Appleton. "Business Cycles and the Modern Theory of Employment," American Economic Review, XXXVI (June, 1946), 278-91.

Meyer, John Robert, and Edwin Kuh. "Acceleration and Related Theories of Investment: an Empirical Inquiry," Review of Economics and Statistics, XXXVII (August, 1955), 217-30.

Miller, Adolph Caspar. "Responsibility for Federal Reserve Policies: 1927-29," American Economic Review, XXV (September, 1935), 442-58.

Minsky, Hyman Philip. "A Linear Model of Cyclical Growth," Review of Economics and Statistics, XLI (May, 1959), 133-45.

Mitchell, Wesley Clair. "Business Cycles," Encyclopedia of the Social Sciences, Vol. III. New York: Macmillan Co., 1930.

Murad, Anatol. "Net Investment and Industrial Progress," in Post-Keynesian Economics, Kenneth Kurihara, editor.

Nelson, Richard Robinson. "The Economics of Invention: A Survey of the Literature," Journal of Business, XXXII (April, 1959), 101-27.

Ohlin, Bertil Gotthard. "Some Notes on the Stockholm Theory of Saving and Investments, II," Economic Journal, XLVII (June, 1937), 221-40.

Pigou, Arthur Cecil. "The Classical Stationary State," Economic Journal, LIII (December, 1943), 343-351.

Richardson, George Barclay. "The Growth of Firms: (II) The Limits to a Firm's Rate of Growth," Oxford Economic Papers, XVI (March, 1964), 9-23.

Robinson, Joan. "The Classification of Inventions," Review of Economic Studies, V (February, 1938), 139-42.

_____. "The Production Function," Economic Journal, LXV (March, 1955), 67-71.

Roos, Charles Frederick, "The Demand for Investment Goods," American Economic Review, Supplement, XXXVIII (May, 1948), 311-20.

Rosenberg, Nathan. "Capital Goods, Technology and Economic Growth," Oxford Economic Papers, XV (November, 1963), 217-27.

Samuelson, Paul Anthony. "Interactions between the Multiplier Analysis and the Principle of Acceleration," The Review of Economics and Statistics, XXI (May, 1939), 75-8.

_____, "Parable and Realism in Capital Theory: The Surrogate Production Function," Review of Economic Studies, XXIX (June, 1962), 193-206.

Schmookler, Jacob. "The Changing Efficiency of the American Economy, 1869-1938," Review of Economics and Statistics, XXXIV (August, 1952), 214-31.

Schumpeter, Joseph Alois. "The Analysis of Economic Change," Review of Economics and Statistics, XVII (May, 1935), 2-10.

_____. "The Explanation of the Business Cycle," Economica, VII (December, 1927), 286-311.

Smith, Vernon Lomax. "Problems in Production-Investment Planning Over Time," International Economic Review, I (September, 1960), 198-216.

_____. "The Theory of Investment and Production," Quarterly Journal of Economics, LXXIII (February, 1959), 61-87.

Smithies, Arthur. "Economic Fluctuations and Growth," Econometrica, XXV (January, 1957), 1-52.

_____. "Forecasting Postwar Demand: I," Econometrica, XIII (January, 1945), 1-14.

_____. "Productivity, Real Wages, and Economic Growth," Quarterly Journal of Economics, LXXIV (May, 1960), 189-205.

Solow, Robert Merton. "Technical Change and the Aggregate Production Function," Review of Economics and Statistics, XXXIX (August, 1957), 312-320.

Spiethoff, Arthur. "Krisen," Handworterbuch der Staatswissenchaften, fourth edition, Vol. VI, 1925.

Stern, Ernest Henry. "Capital Requirements in Progressive Economies," Economica, XII (August, 1945), 163-71.

Stigler, George Joseph. "The Division of Labor is Limited by the Extent of the Market," Journal of Political Economy, LIX (June, 1951), 185-93.

Strassman, Wolfgang Paul. "Interrelated Industries and the Rate of Technological Change," Review of Economic Studies, XXVII (October, 1959), 16-22.

Suits, Daniel B., "The Determinants of Consumer Expenditure: A Review of Present Knowledge," in Impacts of Monetary Policy, Commission on Money and Credit. Englewood Cliffs, New Jersey: Prentice-Hall, 1963. Pp. 1-59.

Tinbergen, Jan. "Statistical evidence on the Acceleration Principle," Economica, V (May, 1938), 164-76.

Tintner, Gerhard. "A 'Simple' Theory of Business Fluctuations," Econometrica, X (July-October, 1942), 317-20.

Tsiang, Sho-Chieh. "Accelerator, Theory of the Firm, and the Business Cycle," Quarterly Journal of Economics, LXV (August, 1951), 325-41.

_____. "Rehabilitation of the Time Dimension of Investment in Macrodynamic Analysis," Economica, XVI (August, 1949), 204-17.

Urquhart, Malcolm C. "Capital Accumulation, Technological Change, and Economic Growth," Canadian Journal of Economics, XXV (November, 1959), 411-30.

Usher, Abbot Payson. "Technical Change and Capital Formation," in Capital Formation and Economic Growth, Universities-National Bureau Committee on Economic Research. Princeton: Princeton University Press, 1955.. Pp. 523-50.

Uzawa, Hirofumi. "Neutral Inventions and the Stability of Growth Equilibrium," Review of Economic Studies, XXVIII (February, 1961), 117-24.

Vanek, Jaroslav. "The Labor Market, Technology, and Stability in the Keynesian Model," Kyklos, XVI (fasc. 1, 1963), 111-20.

_____. "A Theory of Growth with Technological Change," American Economic Review, LVII (March, 1967), 73-89.

_____. "Towards a More General Theory of Growth with Technological Change," Economic Journal, LXXVI (December, 1966), 841-54.

Walters, Alan A. "Production and Cost Functions: an Econometric Survey (with bibliography)," Econometrica, XXXI (January, 1963), 1-66.

B. BOOKS

Ackley, Gardner. Macroeconomic Theory. New York: the Macmillan Company, 1961.

Allen, Frederick Lewis. The Big Change: America Transforms Itself 1900-1950. New York: Harper and Row, 1952.

_____. Only Yesterday. New York: Harper and Row, 1964.

Allen, R. G. D. Macro-economic Theory. New York: St. Martin's Press, 1968.

Bain, Joe Staten. Industrial Organization. New York: Wiley, 1959.

Barger, Harold. The Management of Money. Chicago: Rand, McNally and Co., 1964.

Beveridge, Sir William Henry. Unemployment: A Problem of Industry. London: Longmans, Green & Co., Inc., 1909.

Border, Neil Hopper. The Economic Effects of Advertising. Chicago: Irwin, 1944.

Boulding, Kenneth Ewart. The Organizational Revolution. New York: Harper and Bros.; 1953.

Brooman, Frederick and Henry D. Jacoby. Macroeconomics: An Introduction to Theory and Policy. Chicago: Aldine Publishing Co., 1970.

Brown, Murray. On the Theory and Measurement of Technological Change. Cambridge: Cambridge University Press, 1966.

Burns, Arthur R. The Decline of Competition. New York: McGraw-Hill Book Co., 1936.

Burns, Arthur Frank. The Frontiers of Economic Knowledge; Essays. New York: Princeton University Press, 1954.

Carter, Charles Frederick and Bruce Rodda Williams. Industry and Technical Progress. London: Oxford University Press, 1957.

_____. Investment in Innovation. London: Oxford University Press, 1958.

_____. Science in Industry. London: Oxford University Press, 1959.

Cassel, Gustav. Theory of Social Economy. New York: Harcourt, Brace & Co., Inc., 1923.

Chandler, Alfred Dupont, comp. and editor. Giant Enterprise, Ford, General Motors and the Automobile Industry. New York: Harcourt, Brace and World, 1964.

Chiang, Alpha C. Fundamental Methods of Mathematical Economics. New York: McGraw-Hill, 1967.

Commager, Henry Steele. The American Mind. New Haven: Yale University Press, 1950.

Davidson, Paul and Eugene Smolensky. Aggregate Supply and Demand Analysis. New York: Harper and Row, Publishers, 1964.

233

Denison, Edward. The Sources of Economic Growth in the United States and the Alternatives Before Us. New York: Committee for Economic Development, 1962.

Duesenberry, James. Business Cycles and Economic Growth. New York: McGraw-Hill Book Co., 1958.

_____. Income, Saving, and the Theory of Consumer Behavior. Cambridge: Harvard University Press, 1952.

Epstein, Ralph C. The Automobile Industry: Its Economic and Commercial Development. Chicago: A. W. Shaw Co., 1928.

Evans, Michael K. Macroeconomic Activity: Theory, Forecasting, and Control. New York: Harper and Row, 1969.

Fabricant, Solomon. Basic Facts on Productivity Change. New York: Columbia University Press, 1959.

Faulkner, Harold Underwood. The Decline of Laissez Faire, 1897-1917. New York: Holt, Rinehart and Winston, 1951.

Ferguson, Charles E. The Neoclassical Theory of Production and Distribution. Cambridge: Cambridge University Press, 1969.

Foster, William Trufant and Waddill Catchings. The Road to Plenty. Boston: Houghton Mifflin Co., 1928.

_____. Profits. Boston: Houghton, Mifflin Co., 1925.

_____. Money. Boston: Houghton Mifflin Co., 1923.

Friedman, Milton. A Theory of the Consumption Function. Princeton, New Jersey: Princeton University Press, 1957.

_____, and Anna J. Schwartz. A Monetary History of the United States, 1867-1960. Princeton, New Jersey: Princeton University Press, 1963.

Gordon, Robert A. Business Fluctuations. New York: Harper and Row, 1961.

Gourvitch, Alexander. A Survey of Economic Theory on Technological Change and Employment. New York: Augustus M. Kelley, 1966.

Green, H. A. Aggregation in Economic Analysis. Princeton: Princeton University Press, 1964.

Haberler, Gottfried. Prosperity and Depression. Geneva: League of Nations, 1941.

Hansen, Alvin H. Business Cycles and National Income.
New York: W. W. Norton, 1951.

_____. Fiscal Policy and Business Cycles. New York:
W. W. Norton, 1941.

Hawtrey, Ralph George. The Art of Central Banking. London:
Longmans, Green & Co., 1933.

_____. Capital and Employment. London: Longmans, Green & Co.,
1937.

_____. Currency and Credit. London: Longmans, Green & Co., 1928.

_____. Good and Bad Trade. London: Constable & Co., 1913.

_____. Monetary Reconstruction. New York: Longmans, Green &
Co., 1926.

Hayek, Friedrich August von. Monetary Theory and the Trade
Cycle. New York: Harcourt, Brace & Co., Inc., 1933.

_____. Prices and Production. London: George Routledge &
Sons, Ltd., 1935.

_____. Profits, Interest and Investment. London: George
Routledge & Sons, Ltd., 1939.

_____. Hession, Charles H. and Hyman Sardy. Ascent to
Affluence, A History of American Economic Development.
Boston: Allyn and Bacon, Inc., 1969.

Hicks, John R. A Contribution to the Theory of the Trade
Cycle. Oxford: Clarendon Press, 1950.

_____. The Theory of Wages, Second Edition. New York:
St. Martin's Press, 1966.

Hill, Frank Ernest and Allan Nevins. Ford: The Times, the Man,
the Company. Vol. 1. New York: Scribner's, 1954.

Hultgren, Thor. American Transportation in Prosperity and
Depression. New York: National Bureau of Economic
Research, 1948.

Jerome, Harry. Mechanization in Industry. New York: National
Bureau of Economic Research, 1934.

Jones, Eliot. The Trust Problem in the United States. New York:
Macmillan, 1921.

Keiser, Norman F. Macroeconomics. New York: Random House, 1971.

Kemmerer, Donald Lorenzo and Edwin Walter Kemmerer. The ABC of the Federal Reserve System. New York: Harper and Bros., 1950.

Kendrick, John W. Productivity Trends in the United States. Princeton: Princeton University Press, 1961.

Keynes, John Maynard. The General Theory of Employment, Interest and Money. New York: Harcourt, Brace & World, Inc., 1964.

Kirkland, Edward C. A History of American Economic Life. New York: F. S. Crofts & Co., 1940.

Klein, Lawrence R. An Introduction to Econometrics. Englewood Cliffs, New Jersey: Prentice-Hall, Inc., 1962.

_____, and Arthur Stanley Goldberger. An Econometric Model of the United States, 1929-1952. Amsterdam: North Holland Publishing Co., 1955.

Kogiku, K. C. An Introduction to Macroeconomic Models. New York: McGraw Hill, 1968.

Krooss, Herman E. and Paul Studenski. Financial History of the United States. New York: McGraw-Hill Co., 1952.

Lave, Lester. Technological Change: Its Conception and Measurement. Englewood Cliffs, New Jersey: Prentice-Hall, Inc.,1966.

Lavington, Frederick. The Trade Cycle. An Account of the Causes producing Rhythmical Changes in the Activity of Business. London: P. S. King & Son, Ltd., 1922.

Lee, Maurice W. Macroeconomics: Fluctuations, Growth, and Stability. Homewood, Illinois: Richard D. Irwin, 1971.

Leuchtenberg, William Edward. The Perils of Prosperity, 1914-1932. Chicago: University of Chicago Press, 1958.

Lindauer, John. Macroeconomics. New York: John Wiley & Sons, 1968.

Long, Clarence Dickinson, Jr. Building Cycles and the Theory of Investment. Princeton, New Jersey: Princeton University Press, 1940.

McKenna, Joseph P. Aggregate Economic Analysis. Third Edition. New York: Holt, Rinehart and Winston/The Dryden Press, 1969.

Meyer, John Robert and Edwin Kuh. The Investment Decision. Cambridge: Harvard University Press, 1957.

Mitchell, Wesley Clair. The Backward Art of Spending Money and Other Essays. New York: McGraw-Hill Book Co., 1937.

_____. Business Cycles. Berkeley: University of California Press, 1913.

_____. Business Cycles: The Problem and Its Setting. New York: National Bureau of Economic Research, 1927.

_____. What Happens during Business Cycles. New York: National Bureau of Economic Research, 1951.

Nelson, Ralph Lowell. Merger Movements in American Industry, 1895-1956. Princeton, New Jersey: Princeton University Press, 1959.

Pigou, Arthur Cecil. Economics of Welfare. London: Macmillan & Co., Ltd., 1920.

_____. Industrial Fluctuation. London: Macmillan & Co., 1927.

Robertson, Dennis H. A Study of Industrial Fluctuations. London: P. S. King & Son, Ltd., 1915.

Rostow, Walter W. The Stages of Economic Growth. New York: Cambridge University Press, 1960.

Salter, W. E. G. Productivity and Technical Change. Cambridge: Cambridge University Press, 1960.

Schumpeter, Joseph A. Business Cycles. New York: McGraw-Hill Book Co., 1939.

_____. The Theory of Economic Development. New York: Oxford University Press, 1961.

Shapiro, Edward. Macroeconomic Analysis. Second Edition. New York: Harcourt, Brace & World, Inc., 1970.

Smith, Vernon. Investment and Production: A Study in the Theory of the Capital-Using Enterprise. Cambridge: Harvard University Press, 1966.

Smith, Warren L. Macroeconomics. Homewood, Illinois: Irwin, 1970.

Soule, George. Prosperity Decade: From War to Depression, 1917-1929. New York: Harper & Row, 1968.

Sprinkel, Beryl Wayne. Money and Markets, A Monetarist View. Homewood, Illinois: Richard D. Irwin, Inc., 1971.

Taussig, Principles of Economics. Second Edition. New York: Macmillan Co., 1916.

Taylor, Frederick Winslow. The Principles of Scientific Management. New York: W. W. Norton, 1967, ᶜ1947.

Tinbergen, Jan. Business Cycles in the United States, 1919-1932. Geneva: League of Nations, 1939.

Warburton, Clark. Depression, Inflation, and Monetary Policy: Selected Papers, 1945-1953. Baltimore: Johns Hopkins University Press, 1966.

Weintraub, Sidney. An Approach to the Theory of Income Distribution. Philadelphia: Chilton, 1958.

Wicksell, Kunt. Lectures on Political Economy. London: Routledge and Kegan Paul, 1934.

Wilson, Thomas. Fluctuations in Income and Employment. Third Edition. London: Pittman, 1948.

C. COLLECTED ESSAYS

American Economic Association, Editor. Readings in Business Cycle Theory. Homewood, Illinois: Richard D. Irwin, 1951.

_____, Editor. Readings in Business Cycles. Homewood, Illinois: Richard D. Irwin, 1965.

Duesenberry, James and Gary Fromm, Lawrence Klein, Edwin Kuh, Editors. The Brookings Quarterly Econometric Model of the United States. Chicago: Rand McNally and Co., 1965.

Essays in Honor of Gustav Cassel. London: George Allen and Unwin, Ltd., 1933.

Fellner, William and B. F. Haley, Editors. Readings in the Theory of Income Distribution. Philadelphia: Blakiston Co., 1946.

Hansen, Alvin H. and Richard V. Clemence, Editors. Readings in Business Cycles and National Income. New York: W. W. Norton and Co., Inc., 1953.

Income, Employment and Public Policy: Essays in Honor of Alvin H. Hansen. New York: W. W. Norton, 1948.

Lundberg, Erik, Editor. The Business Cycle in the Post-war World. London: Macmillan and Co., Ltd., 1955.

Mowry, George E., Editor. The Twenties, Fords, Flappers and Fanatics. Englewood Cliffs, New Jersey: Prentice-Hall, 1963.

Mueller, M. G., Editor. Readings in Macroeconomics. New York: Holt, Rinehart and Winston, Inc., 1967.

Nelson, Richard, Editor. Rate and Direction of Inventive Activity. National Bureau of Economic Research. Princeton: Princeton University Press, 1962.

Sen, A., Editor. Growth Economics. Baltimore: Penguin Books, 1970.

Shapiro, Edward, Editor. Macroeconomics: Selected Readings. New York: Harcourt, Brace & World, Inc., 1970.

Shell, Karl, Editor. Essays on the Theory of Optimal Economic Growth. Cambridge: The M. I. T. Press, 1967.

Stiglitz, J. E. and H. Uzawa, Editors. Readings in the Modern Theory of Economic Growth. Cambridge: The M. I. T. Press, 1969.

Zellner, Arnold, Editor. Readings in Economic Statistics and Econometrics. Boston: Little, Brown and Company, 1968.

APPENDIX A

SUPPLEMENTARY TABLES

TABLE I.

FACTOR SHARES, SELECTED YEARS,
1889 - 1957.

Year	Capital's Share	Labor's Share
1889[a]	.3010	.6990
1894	.2975	.7025
1899	.2940	.7060
1904	.2905	.7095
1909	.2870	.7130
1914	.2835	.7165
1919[a]	.2800	.7200
1924	.2785	.7215
1929[a]	.2770	.7230
1934	.2360	.7640
1937[a]	.2120	.7880
1939	.2170	.7830
1944	.2290	.7710
1948[a]	.2380	.7620
1949	.2320	.7680
1954	.2030	.7970
1957[a]	.1860	.8140

[a]These estimates are taken from Kendrick, the remainder
are simply extrapolations. J. Kendrick, Productivity Trends
in the United States (Princeton: Princeton University Press,
1961), Table 28, p. 121.

TABLE II.

NATIONAL ECONOMY: REAL NET PER-CAPITAL OUTPUT, INPUTS, AND
   PRODUCTIVITY RATIOS, KUZNETS CONCEPT, NATIONAL
   SECURITY VERSION, SELECTED YEARS, 1889-1957.
                  (1929 = 100)

Year	Output per Labor Input X*	Capital Input K	Labor Input L	Capital-Labor Ratio	Total Factor Productivity
1889	49.5	25.5	43.4	58.8	57.5
1899	60.5	38.7	55.4	69.9	33.7
1909	69.1	55.7	73.5	75.8	74.8
1919	83.2	76.7	88.7	86.5	86.7
1929	100.0	100.0	100.0	100.0	100.0
1939	114.7	95.8	89.7	106.8	113.0
1947	135.5	108.9	118.2	92.1	138.0
1949	140.2	120.5	114.8	105.0	138.9
1953	158.4	141.6	129.9	109.0	155.5
1957	173.3	160.4	129.4	124.0	165.0

        Data taken from Kendrick, op. cit., Table A-XIX,
pp. 327-330.

TABLE III.

PRIVATE DOMESTIC ECONOMY: REAL GROSS PRODUCT PER-CAPITA,
INPUTS, AND PRODUCTIVITY RATIOS, COMMERCE CONCEPT,
SELECTED YEARS, 1889-1957.
(1929 = 100)

Year	Output per Labor Input X/L	Capital Input K	Labor Input L	Capital- Labor Ratio	Total Factor Productivity
1889	50.0	29.8	44.6	66.8	56.0
1899	61.0	44.4	56.7	78.3	65.4
1909	69.6	61.8	74.9	82.5	73.4
1919	80.4	80.3	86.7	92.6	82.1
1929	100.0	100.0	100.0	100.0	100.0
1939	123.6	94.3	84.2	112.0	120.2
1947	142.3	107.3	110.6	97.0	143.1
1949	152.8	118.1	106.6	110.8	149.3
1953	173.1	139.6	117.2	119.1	166.4
1957	192.6	158.2	116.9	135.3	179.4

Kendrick, op. cit., Table A-XXII, pp.333-335.

TABLE IV.

NATIONAL ECONOMY, KUZNETS CONCEPT, GROWTH RATES FOR
PER-CAPITA OUTPUT, CAPITAL-LABOR RATIO, AND
TECHNICAL CHANGE, SELECTED YEARS, 1889-1957.

Time-Period	$x*$[1]	$k*$[2]	a_e[3]	a[4]	p[5]	γ[6]
1889-1919	1.75%	1.30%	1.23%	1.36%	1.38%	-0.50
1919-1953	1.91	0.68	1.45	1.74	1.73	-1.62
1947-1957	2.49	3.01	1.97	1.85	1.80	+0.66
1889-1899	2.03	1.74	1.43	1.51	1.54	-0.41
1899-1909	1.34	0.81	0.95	1.10	1.11	-0.75
1909-1919	1.87	1.33	1.34	1.49	1.49	-0.75
1919-1929	1.86	1.46	1.34	1.45	1.44	-0.55
1929-1939	1.38	0.66	1.05	1.22	1.23	-0.94
1939-1949	2.03	-0.17	1.57	2.07	2.09	-2.85
1949-1957	2.68	2.10	2.13	2.25	2.18	-0.73

[1]Rate of growth of per-capita income; [2]rate of growth of
capital-labor ratio; [3]Vanek's "equilibrium equation" rate of
growth, $a_e = x*\phi_N$; [4]Hicks neutral rate of technical progress,
$a = x* - \phi_K k*$; [5]rate of growth of total factor productivity;
[6]estimated difference between the rate of growth of capital and
the asymptotic rate of growth of capital, $\gamma = (k*-x*)/\phi_N$.
Data derived from Appendix A, Table II, p. 241.

TABLE V.

PRIVATE DOMESTIC ECONOMY, COMMERCE CONCEPT,
GROWTH RATES FOR PER-CAPITA OUTPUT,
CAPITAL-LABOR RATIO, AND TECHNICAL
CHANGE, SELECTED YEARS, 1889-1957.

Time-Period	$x*^1$	$k*^2$	a_e^3	a^4	p^5	γ^6
1889-1919	1.60%	1.09%	1.13%	1.28%	1.28%	-0.72
1919-1953	2.28	0.74	1.72	2.10	2.10	-2.03
1947-1957	3.07	3.38	2.44	2.37	2.29	+0.39
1889-1899	2.01	1.60	1.41	1.53	1.56	-0.58
1899-1909	1.33	0.52	0.94	1.18	1.16	-1.14
1909-1919	1.45	1.16	1.04	1.12	1.13	-0.40
1919-1929	2.21	0.77	1.59	2.00	1.99	-2.00
1929-1939	2.14	1.14	1.63	1.87	1.86	-1.31
1939-1949	2.14	-0.11	1.65	2.17	2.19	-2.92
1949-1957	2.94	2.53	2.33	2.42	2.32	-0.51

Rates of growth of [1]per-capita income, [2]capital-labor ratio,
[3]Vanek's "equilibrium equation," [4]Hicks neutral technical progress,
[5]total factor productivity. [6]Estimated difference between the
rate of growth of capital and the asymptotic rate of growth of
capital, $\gamma = (k*-x*)/\phi_N$. Data derived from Appendix A, Table III.

APPENDIX B

PROFIT AND COST EQUATIONS

Comparative Static Properties of the Capital-Output Ratio

Assume that the production function takes the Cobb-Douglas form given by (A1). The equation of a given isoquant

(A1) $\qquad X = AK^{\alpha}L^{\beta}$

is specified by (A2). If both factors are paid their marginal

(A2) $\qquad K = L^{-\beta/\alpha}\,(X/A)^{1/\alpha}$

products, then the factor price ratio will be equal to the slope of the isoquant, (A3). The relationship between K and L when an

(A3) $\qquad -\dfrac{dK}{dL} = \dfrac{\alpha L}{\beta W} = \dfrac{R}{W}$

economy is on the expansion path is obtained by solving (A3) for K:

(A4) $\qquad K = \rho L \qquad\qquad$ where $\rho = \dfrac{\alpha W}{\beta R}$

Using the value of K given in (A4), the optimal labor input in terms of factor prices and technology can be obtained by using (A1):

(A5) $\qquad L* = X/A\rho^{\alpha} \qquad$ (Assuming C.R.T.S.)

Equations (A4) and (A5) can be combined to determine the optimum capital input, (A6). The desired capital-output ratio, $\underline{v}$, can be

(A6) $\qquad K* = \rho^{\beta}X/A$

expressed as a function of factor prices and technology:

(A7) $\qquad v = \left(\dfrac{\alpha W}{\beta R}\right)^{\beta}/A$

The desired comparative static properties are given in equations (A8) through (A12):

(A8) $\qquad \dfrac{\delta v}{\delta \alpha} = \dfrac{\beta}{\alpha}\,v > 0$

(A9) $\qquad \dfrac{\delta v}{\delta \beta} = \left(\,\ln\left(\dfrac{\gamma W}{R}\right) + \ln\left(\dfrac{1}{\beta}\right) - 1\right)v \gtrless 0$

(A10) $\dfrac{\delta v}{\delta A} = -\dfrac{1}{A} v < 0$

(A11) $\dfrac{\delta v}{\delta W} = \dfrac{\beta}{W} v > 0$

(A12) $\dfrac{\delta v}{\delta R} = -\dfrac{\beta}{R} v < 0$

The Aggregate Supply Curve

Firms will produce where the marginal revenue product of labor is just equal to the money wage rate, (A13). Solving

(A13) $W = P\beta X/L$

equation (A13) for P, the price level, yields an expression in terms of both output and labor. To eliminate the labor term,

(A14) $P = WL/\beta X$

equation (A1) is solved for L, assuming that the capital stock is fixed at K_o, (A15), and substituted into (A14) to arrive at

(A15) $L = (X/AK_o^{\alpha})^{1/\beta}$

the aggregate supply curve, equation (A16). The first and second derivatives of (A16) are computed to determine the slope and curvature of the aggregate supply curve.

(A16) $P = \dfrac{W}{\beta} \gamma X^{\alpha/\beta}$ where $\gamma = (AK_o^{\alpha})^{-1/\beta}$

(A17) $\dfrac{\delta P}{\delta X} = (\dfrac{1}{\beta}-1)\dfrac{W}{\beta}\gamma X^{(\frac{1}{\beta}-2)} > 0$

(A18) $\dfrac{\delta^2 P}{\delta X^2} = (\dfrac{1}{\beta}-2)(\dfrac{1}{\beta}-1)\dfrac{\gamma W}{\beta} X^{(\frac{1}{\beta}-3)} < 0$

Cost Curves

The total cost of production will be given by (A19).

(A19) $\qquad TC = W_o L + RK_o$

To express total cost as a function of output, the term L is replaced with its equivalent expression (A15):

(A20) $\qquad TC(X) = W_o \gamma X^{(1/\beta)} + RK_o$

Marginal cost is calculated from (A20) and is identical to the aggregate supply curve derived in (A16). Average cost is

(A21) $\qquad MC(X) = \frac{W\gamma}{\beta} X^{(\alpha/\beta)}$

obtained by dividing (A20) by X. The point of minimum average cost is then calculated by taking the derivative of (A22) with

(A22) $\qquad AC(X) = W\gamma X^{(\alpha/\beta)} + RK_o X^{-1}$

respect to X and equating it to zero. The output for which

$$\frac{dAC(X)}{dX} = \frac{\alpha W\gamma X^{(\alpha/\beta)}}{\beta X} - RK_o X^{-2} = 0$$

(A23) $\qquad X = AK_o \rho^{-\beta}$

average cost is minimized is given in (A23). Note that if this relationship is inverted and solved for K, the relationship between the capital stock and the optimal rate of output is obtained, equation (A24).

(A24) $\qquad K = \rho^\beta XA^{-1}$ $\qquad\qquad$ (compare with (A6))

There are two ways to determine the value of minimum average cost. Minimum average cost will be the long-run average cost, (A25), where L* and K* represent the optimal factor inputs.

(A25) $\qquad LRAC(X) = WL*X^{-1} + RK*X^{-1}$

Substituting the values of the optimal inputs given earlier
by equations (A5) and (A6) and simplifying gives long-run
average cost in terms of factor prices and technology:

(A26) $\qquad \text{LRAC}(X) = A^{-1}(\frac{W}{\beta})^{\beta}(\frac{R}{\gamma})^{\alpha}$

Another approach could have been to substitute the value of X
obtained in (A23) into the average cost function (A22). The
result, of course, would be identical to that obtained in (A26).

The average profit of production is the difference between
the price level and the average cost. Subtracting (A16) from (A22):

(A27) $\qquad A\pi = \frac{WYX^{(\alpha/\beta)}}{\beta} - WYX^{(\alpha/\beta)} - RKX^{-1} = \frac{WY\alpha}{\beta}X^{(\alpha/\beta)} - RKX^{-1}$

Total profit is obtained by multiplying (A27) by X:

(A28) $\qquad T\pi = \frac{WY\alpha}{\beta}X^{(1/\beta)} - RK$

Equation (A28) represents the total profit being earned at
an output of X units and a capital stock of K units. To examine
the change in profit when the capital stock is changed, imagine
that firms expect the price level to remain unchanged, or at
least, that they have no control over the price level. Profits
will be maximized by minimizing costs. Potential profit in the
economy is given by total revenue minus total cost. Total
revenue is given by PX where P is calculated on the basis of the
current price level, (A29). The total cost will depend on the

(A29) $\qquad TR = WX^{1/\beta}/A^{\beta}K_{0}^{\alpha}$

the anticipated capital stock, K. Total profit as a function of the capital stock is given by equation (A31).

(A30) $TC = W(\frac{X}{A})^{(1/\beta)} K^{-\gamma/\beta} + RK$

(A31) $\pi(K) = W(\frac{X}{A})^{1/\beta} (\frac{1}{\beta}K_o^{-\alpha/\beta} - K^{-\alpha/\beta}) - RK$

Equation (A31) gives the profitability function as dependent on the existing stock of capital, K_o, and any other capital stock, K, and the current rate of output, X. To examine the slope and curvature, the first and second derivatives are computed:

(A32) $\pi'(K) = \frac{W\gamma}{\beta}(\frac{X}{AK})^{1/\beta} - R > 0$ if $K < K^*$

(A33) $\pi''(K) = -\frac{\alpha W}{\beta^2} (\frac{X}{A})^{1/\beta} K^{-(1+\beta)/\beta} < 0$

To calculate the capital stock for which profits are maximized, (A31) is differentiated with respect to capital and set equal to zero. The capital stock which maximizes profits is simply the desired capital stock given by (A6).

Dissertations in American Economic History

An Arno Press Collection

1977 Publications

Ankli, Robert Eugene. **Gross Farm Revenue in Pre-Civil War Illinois.** (Doctoral Dissertation, University of Illinois, 1969). 1977

Asher, Ephraim. **Relative Productivity, Factor-Intensity and Technology in the Manufacturing Sectors of the U.S. and the U.K. During the Nineteenth Century.** (Doctoral Dissertation, University of Rochester, 1969). 1977

Campbell, Carl. **Economic Growth, Capital Gains, and Income Distribution: 1897-1956.** (Doctoral Dissertation, University of California at Berkeley, 1964). 1977

Cederberg, Herbert R. **An Economic Analysis of English Settlement in North America, 1583-1635.** (Doctoral Dissertation, University of California at Berkeley, 1968). 1977

Dente, Leonard A. **Veblen's Theory of Social Change.** (Doctoral Dissertation, New York University, 1974). 1977

Dickey, George Edward. **Money, Prices and Growth;** The American Experience, 1869-1896. (Doctoral Dissertation, Northwestern University, 1968). 1977

Douty, Christopher Morris. **The Economics of Localized Disasters:** The 1906 San Francisco Catastrophe. (Doctoral Dissertation, Stanford University, 1969). 1977

Harper, Ann K. **The Location of the United States Steel Industry, 1879-1919.** (Doctoral Dissertation, Johns Hopkins University, 1976). 1977

Holt, Charles Frank. **The Role of State Government in the Nineteenth-Century American Economy, 1820-1902:** A Quantitative Study. (Doctoral Dissertation, Purdue University, 1970). 1977

Katz, Harold. **The Decline of Competition in the Automobile Industry, 1920-1940.** (Doctoral Dissertation, Columbia University, 1970). 1977

Lee, Susan Previant. **The Westward Movement of the Cotton Economy, 1840-1860:** Perceived Interests and Economic Realities. (Doctoral Dissertation, Columbia University, 1975). 1977

Legler, John Baxter. **Regional Distribution of Federal Receipts and Expenditures in the Nineteenth Century:** A Quantitative Study. (Doctoral Dissertation, Purdue University, 1967). 1977

Lightner, David L. **Labor on the Illinois Central Railroad, 1852-1900:** The Evolution of an Industrial Environment. (Doctoral Dissertation, Cornell University, 1969). 1977

MacMurray, Robert R. **Technological Change in the American Cotton Spinning Industry, 1790 to 1836.** (Doctoral Dissertation, University of Pennsylvania, 1970). 1977

Netschert, Bruce Carlton. **The Mineral Foreign Trade of the United States in the Twentieth Century:** A Study in Mineral Economics. (Doctoral Dissertation, Cornell University, 1949). 1977

Otenasek, Mildred. **Alexander Hamilton's Financial Policies.** (Doctoral Dissertation, Johns Hopkins University, 1939). 1977

Parks, Robert James. **European Origins of the Economic Ideas of Alexander Hamilton.** (M. A. Thesis, Michigan State University, 1963). 1977

Parsons, Burke Adrian. **British Trade Cycles and American Bank Credit:** Some Aspects of Economic Fluctuations in the United States, 1815-1840. (Doctoral Dissertation, University of Texas, 1958). 1977

Primack, Martin L. **Farm Formed Capital in American Agriculture, 1850-1910.** (Doctoral Dissertation, University of North Carolina, 1963). 1977

Pritchett, Bruce Michael. **A Study of Capital Mobilization, The Life Insurance Industry of the Nineteenth Century.** (Doctoral Dissertation, Purdue University, 1970). Revised Edition. 1977

Prosper, Peter A., Jr. **Concentration and the Rate of Change of Wages in the United States, 1950-1962.** (Doctoral Dissertation, Cornell University 1970). 1977

Schachter, Joseph. **Capital Value and Relative Wage Effects of Immigration into the United States, 1870-1930.** (Doctoral Dissertation, City University of New York, 1969). 1977

Schaefer, Donald Fred. **A Quantitative Description and Analysis of the Growth of the Pennsylvania Anthracite Coal Industry, 1820 to 1865.** (Doctoral Dissertation, University of North Carolina, 1967). 1977

Schmitz, Mark. **Economic Analysis of Antebellum Sugar Plantations in Louisiana.** (Doctoral Dissertation, University of North Carolina, 1974). 1977

Sharpless, John Burk, II. **City Growth in the United States, England and Wales, 1820-1861:** The Effects of Location, Size and Economic Structure on Inter-urban Variations in Demographic Growth. (Doctoral Dissertation, University of Michigan, 1975). 1977

Shields, Roger Elwood. **Economic Growth with Price Deflation, 1873-1896.** (Doctoral Dissertation, University of Virginia, 1969). 1977

Stettler, Henry Louis, III. **Growth and Fluctuations in the Ante-Bellum Textile Industry.** (Doctoral Dissertation, Purdue University, 1970). 1977

Sturm, James Lester. **Investing in the United States, 1798-1893:** Upper Wealth-Holders in a Market Economy. (Doctoral Dissertation, University of Wisconsin, 1969). 1977

Tenenbaum, Marcel. **(A Demographic Analysis of Interstate Labor Growth Rate Differentials;** United States, 1890-1900 to 1940-50. (Doctoral Dissertation, Columbia University, 1969). 1977

Thomas, Robert Paul. **An Analysis of the Pattern of Growth of the Automobile Industry:** 1895-1929. (Doctoral Dissertation, Northwestern University, 1965). 1977

Vickery, William Edward. **The Economics of the Negro Migration 1900-1960.** (Doctoral Dissertation, University of Chicago, 1969). 1977

Waters, Joseph Paul. **Technological Acceleration and the Great Depression.** (Doctoral Dissertation, Cornell University, 1971). 1977

Whartenby, Franklee Gilbert. **Land and Labor Productivity in United States Cotton Production, 1800-1840.** (Doctoral Dissertation, University of North Carolina, 1963). 1977

1975 Publications

Adams, Donald R., Jr. **Wage Rates in Philadelphia, 1790-1830.** (Doctoral Dissertation, University of Pennsylvania, 1967). 1975

Aldrich, Terry Mark. **Rates of Return on Investment in Technical Education in the Ante-Bellum American Economy.** (Doctoral Dissertation, The University of Texas at Austin, 1969). 1975

Anderson, Terry Lee. **The Economic Growth of Seventeenth Century New England:** A Measurement of Regional Income. (Doctoral Dissertation, University of Washington, 1972). 1975

Bean, Richard Nelson. **The British Trans-Atlantic Slave Trade, 1650-1775.** (Doctoral Dissertation, University of Washington, 1971). 1975

Brock, Leslie V. **The Currency of the American Colonies, 1700-1764:** A Study in Colonial Finance and Imperial Relations. (Doctoral Dissertation University of Michigan, 1941). 1975

Ellsworth, Lucius F. **Craft to National Industry in the Nineteenth Century:** A Case Study of the Transformation of the New York State Tanning Industry. (Doctoral Dissertation, University of Delaware, 1971). 1975

Fleisig, Heywood W. **Long Term Capital Flows and the Great Depression:** The Role of the United States, 1927-1933. (Doctoral Dissertation, Yale University, 1969). 1975

Foust, James D. **The Yeoman Farmer and Westward Expansion of U.S. Cotton Production.** (Doctoral Dissertation, University of North Carolina at Chapel Hill, 1968). 1975

Golden, James Reed. **Investment Behavior By United States Railroads, 1870-1914.** (Doctoral Thesis, Harvard University, 1971). 1975

Hill, Peter Jensen. **The Economic Impact of Immigration into the United States.** (Doctoral Dissertation, The University of Chicago, 1970). 1975

Klingaman, David C. **Colonial Virginia's Coastwise and Grain Trade.** (Doctoral Dissertation, University of Virginia, 1967). 1975

Lang, Edith Mae. **The Effects of Net Interregional Migration on Agricultural Income Growth:** The United States, 1850-1860. (Doctoral Thesis, The University of Rochester, 1971). 1975

Lindley, Lester G. **The Constitution Faces Technology:** The Relationship of the National Government to the Telegraph, 1866-1884. (Doctoral Thesis, Rice University, 1971). 1975

Lorant, John H[erman]. **The Role of Capital-Improving Innovations in American Manufacturing During the 1920's.** (Doctoral Thesis, Columbia University, 1966). 1975

Mishkin, David Joel. **The American Colonial Wine Industry:** An Economic Interpretation, Volumes I and II. (Doctoral Thesis, University of Illinois, 1966). 1975

Winkler, Donald R. **The Production of Human Capital:** A Study of Minority Achievement. (Doctoral Dissertation, University of California at Berkeley, 1972). 1977

Oates, Mary J. **The Role of the Cotton Textile Industry in the Economic Development of the American Southeast:** 1900-1940. (Doctoral Dissertation, Yale University, 1969). 1975

Passell, Peter. **Essays in the Economics of Nineteenth Century American Land Policy.** (Doctoral Dissertation, Yale University, 1970). 1975

Pope, Clayne L. **The Impact of the Ante-Bellum Tariff on Income Distribution.** (Doctoral Dissertation, The University of Chicago, 1972). 1975

Poulson, Barry Warren. **Value Added in Manufacturing, Mining, and Agriculture in the American Economy From 1809 To 1839.** (Doctoral Dissertation, The Ohio State University, 1965). 1975

Rockoff, Hugh. **The Free Banking Era: A Re-Examination.** (Doctoral Dissertation, The University of Chicago, 1972). 1975

Schumacher, Max George. **The Northern Farmer and His Markets During the Late Colonial Period.** (Doctoral Dissertation, University of California at Berkeley, 1948). 1975

Seagrave, Charles Edwin. **The Southern Negro Agricultural Worker:** 1850-1870. (Doctoral Dissertation, Stanford University, 1971). 1975

Solmon, Lewis C. **Capital Formation by Expenditures on Formal Education, 1880 and 1890.** (Doctoral Dissertation, The University of Chicago, 1968). 1975

Swan, Dale Evans. **The Structure and Profitability of the Antebellum Rice Industry:** 1859. (Doctoral Dissertation, University of North Carolina at Chapel Hill, 1972). 1975

Sylla, Richard Eugene. **The American Capital Market, 1846-1914:** A Study of the Effects of Public Policy on Economic Development. (Doctoral Thesis, Harvard University, 1968). 1975

Uselding, Paul John. **Studies in the Technological Development of the American Economy During the First Half of the Nineteenth Century.** (Doctoral Dissertation, Northwestern University, 1970). 1975

Walsh, William D[avid]. **The Diffusion of Technological Change in the Pennsylvania Pig Iron Industry, 1850-1870.** (Doctoral Dissertation, Yale University, 1967). 1975

Weiss, Thomas Joseph. **The Service Sector in the United States, 1839 Through 1899.** (Doctoral Thesis, University of North Carolina at Chapel Hill, 1967). 1975

Zevin, Robert Brooke. **The Growth of Manufacturing in Early Nineteenth Century New England.** 1975